BORN TO BE A MISSIONARY

A book of real miracles and personal experiences in the life of Missionary Melvin H. High Sr.

At the author's request, 50% of royalties due to the author will be put back into the Flame of Truth Ministries, from hence it came, giving the honor and glory to God!!

Acknowledgements

First and Foremost, I give thanks to my Lord Jesus Christ for his infinite love and compassion. For the revelation and inspiration, he gives to us as we travel and minister under the anointing of the Holy Spirit as he chooses. As we minister to the hurting and needy and as God uses us to help people in their dire need in any situation through the Holy Spirit. Not of ourselves lest we should boast. We give all the glory and honor to Christ our Lord and Savior.

I am grateful to my wife Anna for walking beside me all these years, raising our family of twelve children. For encouraging me to continue with this great project of writing this book. Supporting me when I was spending more time with the book, writing late into the night and sometimes into the morning hours, and less time spent with her. For taking care of the finances for the Ministry and our home. Feeding and housing the family as well as the Missionary groups that came to serve on the Mission Field, the house was never empty. At times, taking Missionary groups into Mexico and translating for them in my absence. Faithfully writing and mailing the quarterly newsletter, keeping all supporters informed of the happenings.

Thanks to all my twelve children for following me as I followed Christ. Contributing to the Ministry in their own special way, and some children continuing to help with the Ministry today. Our children are all business minded and quite successful people with a heart of serving others.

I must recognize my spiritual father and mentor, Rev. Luke Weaver from Grace Chapel, who has unselfishly contributed to my spiritual growth and character. When I needed a push to go forward in the kingdom of God, he was always there with sound advice and prayers.

I am especially grateful to all my friends and partners who support this vision with their prayers and financial gifts. It is because of all of you that we were able to do all the work we accomplished through the power of the Holy Spirit. May God reward you abundantly.

Introduction

The book you are about to read is the story of my life as a Missionary as I served Christ. I will take you through memories of my childhood and my early Christian life as God molded me and made me. You will read stories of how God saved my life when Satan tried to steal it thirteen times. God had a plan and purpose for my life, but despite Satan's attempts, death could not take me.

I will be sharing a small portion of the miracles that happened during these 55+ years in our Ministry in Mexico and other Latin American countries we ministered in. I pray this book encourages you and helps to build your faith and trust in our Heavenly Father. I trust it will challenge your heart.

Jesus said in ***John 5:39 Search the scriptures; for in them ye think ye have eternal life: and they are they which testify of me.***
I have added many scripture verses to do my best to explain to you why I and multitudes of others are devoting our lives to the work of the Lord.

Many people say that God does not move in miraculous ways today. I am here to share with you that God has not stopped moving by his Spirit. I and millions of Christians are seeing the Holy Spirit move as we allow him to use us as he desires.

I have tried my best to share the workings of the Holy Spirit in our day and time as to not offend anyone. When I became hungry for more of God as he was dealing with me, I asked Him if He had anything more that I have not yet received, I wanted it now. I have personally received the Baptism of the Holy Spirit even though I was taught that speaking in tongues was of the devil. When someone says that God does not operate in the Gifts of the Spirit today, it is because they have either been taught that way, or they don't understand the scriptures.

God has spoken to me many times to pray and impart the gifts to others. This has proven successful in many areas and countries as you will read in this book. You will read about how God is moving in Argentina as well as in Haiti and Latin America. God is using people marvelously all over the world. I have seen many miracles everywhere I go, even in our homeland, the United States of America (US).

The Lord blessed me with the gift of the Spanish Language, and I have taught Spanish to others. The students would ask me why I had to teach the Spanish language, when all I had to do was pray for them to receive it as I did. There are several people that attended the Spanish classes, that God moved, and you cannot distinguish the difference from their Spanish and a native-born Latin American.

My mission in life is to help others understand the scriptures in a better way. If you need some help in your Church or Bible Study group, to explain the Gift of the Holy Spirit, I am available. I would be glad to sit down with you and expound the scriptures in a more perfect way

If you have a problem about that which is written in this book, first go to God in prayer, he will give you the understanding. Secondly, I am open to God and his people for correction. I encourage you to read the scriptures and ask questions for things you do not understand.

Thank you, and God Bless you!

You can contact me at:
Flame of Truth, 732 El Dora Road, Donna, TX 78537
Email: _mhighsr2002@yahoo.com_

Preface

As I share my experiences in my walk with the Lord, as I was called by the Holy Spirit to be a Missionary to Mexico and Latin America. You may ask me, *"Why do you sometimes refer to the **Holy Ghost** and other times you refer to the **Holy Spirit"**?* Some people get offended if you use one and/or the other. To me, either one refers to the third person in the Godhead bodily. Strong's definition is the same Greek word, **pneuma :** pnyoo'-mah   Holy Ghost **<pneuma>** Verses Holy Spirit **pneuma** Search for 4151 in KJV from 4154; a current of air, i.e. breath (blast) or a breeze; by analogy or figuratively, a spirit, i.e. (human) the rational soul, (by implication) vital principle, mental disposition, etc., or (superhuman) an angel, demon, or (divine) **God, Christ's spirit, the Holy Spirit:--ghost, life, spirit(-ual, -ually), mind.** Compare 5590.

Jesus himself said in:
Matthew 1:18 ¶ Now the birth of Jesus Christ was on this wise: When as his mother Mary was espoused to Joseph, before they came together, she was found with child of the Holy Ghost.

Luke 11:13 If ye then, being evil, know how to give good gifts unto your children: how much more shall your heavenly Father give the Holy Spirit to them that ask him?

Colossians 2:9 For in him dwelleth all the fullness of the Godhead bodily.

Matthew 28:19 Go ye therefore, and teach all nations, baptizing them in the name of the Father, and of the Son, and of the Holy Ghost:

INDEX

CHAPTER 16:
INSTITUTE OF MINISTRY FLIGHTS

CHAPTER 17
THE MINISTRY TODAY

CHAPTER 18
GOD'S CONTINUING HEALING POWER

CHAPTER 19
I KNOW WHO HOLDS TOMORROW

CHAPTER 20
WHO WE ARE, WHAT WE DO, AND WHY

CHAPTER 1
FAMILY HISTORY

ON MY FATHER'S SIDE

My Father was from German Descent. His forefathers migrated from Germany to Switzerland after the Anabaptist movement began in 1525. This was during the time when Luther Zwingli, Martin Luther and many others led their movement away from Catholicism. Many practices were changed but infant baptism, the accepted mode for most of Christian history was not.

At that time the Swiss Church laws were to baptize all infant babies. Two ministers of the Gospel in the State Church named Menno Simon and Martin Luther had the revelation and conviction that infant baptism was not biblical. As the Bible says in ***Acts 2:38 Then Peter said unto them, Repent, and be baptized every one of you in the name of Jesus Christ for the remission of sins, and ye shall receive the gift of the Holy Ghost.*** The two ministers and their followers realized that an infant has neither knowledge of their sins or repentance in their life. So, Baptism should not be performed until after one becomes a Born-Again Christian. This was a radical idea that cut at the heart of both Church and State. Yet it was just one of many revolutionary ideas typical of a diverse group called Anabaptists. Their movement is also known as the Radical Reformation.

This was completely against the State Church laws, and it caused friction in the church. Again, persecution arose. The State Church began to slaughter all the people that they found in this new faith. The Swiss State Church called it heresy. Living in the age of religious pluralism, we wonder why people in the 16th century would be tortured or drowned over the issue of mode of baptism.

People began to flee and search for shelter and protection from their prosecutors. My father was the 6th generation of John High, one of two brothers that came from Switzerland to the United States of America, for freedom of their newfound faith in Jesus Christ. Freedom to worship and follow their God the way the Bible teaches. This was the start of the Mennonite Church.

To learn more about their persecution, read the book of the *"MARTYRS MIRROR". It will open your eyes to the truth of how multitudes of Christians had to suffer and die for their faith in God. The way they killed them was inhumane such as tying them to a stake and burning them alive and holding others under water till they drowned. It was the most horrifying, gruesome story I have ever read. I started getting nauseous, and I was not able to complete it.

I questioned my God, how could anyone do such demonic things to another human being, less yet people that called themselves Christians. I guess you can see that when people get more involved in their religion than salvation, they believe they are doing their God a favor. Any form of religion has seemingly always been one of the most powerful evil forces in the world against true Christianity. We absolutely need true Christianity first, after that you find the church you can believe in and follow Jesus to the best of your knowledge according to the Word of God.

My father's first wife, Amanda Horting, passed away in December 24,1960. My father remarried Amanda Snader on January 1, 1968 and he passed away on September 23, 1973.

ON MY MOTHERS SIDE

My mother also had mostly German heritage. But according to the testimony of my mother and her Sister Sally on their death beds stating that my great-grandfather was a full-blooded Native American Cheraw Indian. There is a town by that name in the northern part of South Carolina right by the Pee-Dee River. We believe that he was adopted or accepted into a German family and took on their family name of Schlott. When the United States made all Native Americans go to the Indian Reservations, he escaped.

His new name was given as, Henry Schlott, He married Mary Ann Gable. They had a daughter, Sarah Ann Schlott who married, John Horting, which was my Grandfather. Sarah Ann and John had a daughter Amanda that married my father John S High, they both have gone on to their eternal reward.

The Mennonite Church did not believe in being involved in politics or bearing arms. During the Revolutionary War, my Great Grand Father Henry Schlott was drafted to go to Chambersburg, PA to help win the war. He refused to bear arms, the army forced him to work to help serve those that did the fighting. After the war was over, they were so happy to welcome him back home.

As far as I know, my father and mother were of the Mennonite faith all their lives. My father became a born-again Christian later in life, I believe in his 60's. He was burning some brush in the garden, when suddenly, he became convicted of his sins. He immediately got rid of his old habit by throwing his smoke pipe and tobacco in the fire. Thank God, he then decided to follow Jesus all the way. As far as I know, my mother was a Christian most of her life, but they continued to attend the Mennonite Church.

I was brought up in a very religious Mennonite Church we were not encouraged to talk about our faith. I was told by the elders that you cannot know that you are saved. You only hope that when you die, you lived a good enough life that your Heavenly Father would let you into Heaven. According to this theory, it is only by works and not by the redemptive work of Jesus Christ on the cross of Calvary that you will be accepted into heaven. I hear now that most of the Mennonite Churches preaches that you must be born again. Thank you, Lord, for revealing yourself to them.
Jesus himself said in:

 John 3:7 Marvel not that I said unto thee, Ye must be born again. {again: or, from above} (KJV.)

 John 3:3 Jesus answered and said unto him, Verily, verily, I say unto thee, except a man be born again, he cannot see the kingdom of God.

 Ephesians 2:8 For by grace are ye saved through faith; and that not of yourselves: it is the gift of God: 9 Not of works, lest any man should boast.

 1 John 5:13 These things have I written unto you that believe on the name of the Son of God; that ye may know that ye have eternal life, and that ye may believe on the name of the Son of God.

According to the Bible you surely must know that you have opened your heart, and accepted Jesus Christ as Lord and Savior of your life. It is not just "I hope so", you must have the experience of accepting him. and know you have been born again.

BORN DURING THE GREAT DEPRESSION

I was Born during the great depression on April 16, 1929 to John S. & Amanda Horting High, I was born in a farmhouse in Brecknock Township, Lancaster County, PA.

During those years work was hard to find. We had no transportation, since we had no money to buy a car. No electricity in the home. We ate mostly whatever we raised in the garden. With food being sparse, having 8 young mouths to feed with little to no money, we had to be creative. The milk in our baby bottles were diluted with water and coffee. Life was very tough.

Life quality was very poor, many people contracted illnesses such as the Scarlet Fever, Malaria, Mumps, Measles, and Diphtheria, and in those days, there were not many cures even for common illnesses like today, so most were life threatening. My sister Anna Mae tells the story that when I was nearly one year old, I became very ill with a high fever. We had no money to go to the doctor, so I was not diagnosed, but she told me that I had such a high fever that I lay in my crib delirious. My mother, father and my sister Anna Mae could not hold me still and I faded to the point of unconsciousness. As Mennonites, we were not taught how to pray, but when all hope was gone, my parents and sister knelt and prayed the best way they could. To their surprise, God gave them a miracle, I immediately started getting better. You see God had a plan for my life, he was not finished with me yet.

We moved to a tenant house near Bowmansville, PA. During this time my father was able to find work with, "Work Progress Administration" (WPA) where he earned .50 cents a day using a shovel, a pick and a sledge hammer, building roads for the State.

Later my father was able to get a job in a stone quarry for .75 cents a day. He soon had enough money to buy an old used car for the family.

That fall my older brothers were sawing and splitting fire wood to heat the house for the winter. As you know, a one-and-a-half-year-old boy will be a boy, I thought I had to be in the middle of everything and wanted to help like a big boy. I came around the side of my brother to pick up the wood he had split and to carry it to my other brother in the barn stacking it to keep it dry for the winter. He didn't see me coming, I bent down to pick up the wood, as my brother was coming down with the ax. The blade penetrated my head opening the skull like a can opener. God was with me.

While I was healing from the head injury, I was playing on the kitchen floor with the wood from the wood box. I was building a log house, when suddenly I said in Pennsylvania

Dutch, "Mam igh cans hols net tzena." Which in English translates to, "Mother I cannot see the wood." My parents rushed me to our family doctor, in Ephrata PA. When he examined me, he said, "A little bit deeper and this boy would not be alive, the lining over the brain was cut." Thank God, he spared my life again. Evidently Satan knew the impact that my life would have for the gospel of Jesus Christ later in life.

Once I healed, my eye sight did come back. I did suffer some damage, I now had to wear glasses, but thank God, I could see.

I was about two years old when most of my siblings and I got the Mumps. I got it on both sides at the same time and mother did not expect me to live. My mother said that I could not swallow water for three days. Us siblings also shared the Chicken Pox close to the same time, I again got a double portion of that.

CHAPTER 2
CHILDHOOD MEMORIES

MOVING ON

Within the first five years of my childhood, our family moved four times. Of which, I have very few memories at such a young age.

We moved into a tenant farmhouse near Brownstown, PA. I remember one time we were playing with the landlord's children in the meadow barefooted. One of the children stepped on a pitch fork. I remember seeing the steel prong sticking out of the top of her foot.

Some time later I was playing outside when suddenly I saw fire billowing out of the roof of the landlord's house, it was struck by lightning and caught on fire. I screamed for help and my parents came to see what was happening. When they saw the fire, they notified the neighbors. Again, we were without a home. The landlord needed the house we were living in since their house was not fit to live in.

Afterwards, we moved into a tenant house near Hinkletown, PA. I remember seeing my father and sister Anna Mae coming home from work one day in the old car. My father stalled the engine at the end of the driveway. The car had no brakes in reverse. Suddenly the car started going backwards down over a very steep bank towards the Conestoga Creek. I was so scared, I ran to the house to tell my mother. I ran back expecting to see them drowned in the creek. Thank God, my father was able to turn the steering wheel enough for the front fender to catch onto a tree that stopped the car. Our neighbors came to the rescue with their old tractor and a cable and pulled the car up the hill. Soon the car was back in the driveway.

One day, my father allowed me to put a fishing line in that same creek overnight. The next day I went to check it. When I saw the line going from side to side, I was so scared and exited at the same time. I did not know what to do. I ran all the way back to the house, up over the bank and across the road and hollered to my sister Anna Mae for help. I yelled, "I caught a big fish!" She grabbed my father's fish net he had made and ran to help me. I ran back over the road and down the bank to the creek as fast as I could, and before my sister could get there, I pulled my first fish onto the bank, it was a big one and I was so proud.

I started school while living near Hinkletown, PA. It was quite difficult for me the first year. I spoke very little English, we only spoke what we called Pennsylvania Dutch (Low German). After one year in school I was able to do quite well learning the English language. I started the second grade there as well. Soon after school started that fall, the landlord's son got married. We had to move again to allow the newlyweds to move in.

We moved to Fairmont, PA temporarily until spring. It was customary for the Mennonites to move in those days in the spring after the weather warmed up and before the crops were planted.

I went to three different schools that same year. We did not know what it was like to stay in one place. For a very long time, life was hard, moving from place to place, having to make new friends, but it was an adventure.

DIAMOND STATION FARM

When I was eight years old, we moved to a farm in Diamond Station, near Ephrata, PA. We lived in a house that the landlord purchased for when one of their children got married. We were able to live there for six years, before their son got married. I had many experiences and great memories while living there. I was able to plant my feet a little and I became a young man and learned to work hard.

We had little money to buy food, so the food we ate was not always the greatest. I knew what it was like to eat corn mush for breakfast, and fried corn mush for dinner made from the leftover corn from the fields after the farmers were done harvesting. We had butter and jelly sandwiches for our school lunches. Sometimes, for a special treat, the chickens laid enough eggs for us to have an egg sandwich.

Soon after we moved there my mother gave birth to a still born son. Later she gave birth to the 14th child, our youngest sister Miriam. She died at the age of two-an-a-half, from Diphtheria. This left us with twelve living brothers and sisters. I was number eight in the family.

A picture of my siblings from the oldest on the right to the youngest
Anna Mae, Paul, Ivan, John David, Henry, Emma (missing), Lydia, Melvin, Christ,
Luke, Jacob, and Mary Helen
My father John and step mother Amanda in the front row.

I remember my father helping my uncle dig a large hole on his farm for a cellar for a new house for his son, which was getting married soon. One Saturday morning my father asked me to go along and help. I needed to ride one of the horse teams pulling a dirt scoop, a much faster way than digging by hand. I pulled the scoop full of dirt out of the hole when the scoop caught up on a rock and flipped. This threw dirt all over the horses, and it spooked them. They started to run out of control. I was so scared, all I could do was hang on for dear life. I could not hang on for long, I slid half way down the side of the horse when the horses made a sharp turn to cross the road and stumbled. I fell off and one of the big horses fell right on top of me, then jumped up and continued to run. My father saw what happened and came running, expecting to find me dead. When my father came near, he saw me getting up. I had fallen into a ditch and the horse's weight did not fully land on me. I did injure my neck from the fall and suffered nerve damage. You see the Lord had a plan for my life. The devil tried to destroy me again, but when God has a plan, even the Devil can't stop it.

My father worked night shift in the Akron Shoe Factory. One night after work, while walking home, he heard a car coming down the road very slowly behind him. He felt very strongly that something was wrong, so he hid in the field. The car stopped close to where he was. He heard the men say, "He was right here, where did he go?" They pulled away but continued to pass by several times very slowly watching for my father to come out of hiding. My father knew that they were planning to rob him, he told us it was the night he had received his pay and was carrying the cash in his pocket. Finally, the men gave up and my father got home safe, just a little later than usual.

Our father worked in several factories during those years. The landlord allowed my father to also grow tobacco on his farm. When the tobacco was sold my father was able to pay the rent for the whole year.

HIT BY A BIG TRUCK

One day my father allowed me to go with him to a public sale in Ephrata, PA. He bought some things and I begged him to allow me to take it to the car across the street. It was winter time, with freezing rain, so everything was icy. I took care crossing the street. When I was returning, I was so excited and forgot to look before crossing the street and ran out in front of a truck. The truck hit me and knocked me down on the icy road. The driver slammed on the brakes and slid the tires which pushed me up the street until it came to a complete stop. I jumped up and ran back to my father, and the driver followed me. He wanted to take me to the doctor. I assured him and my father that I was alright. I really was, thank God, another miracle. I could have been killed by the truck as easy as not. Devil you missed again.

One day us four younger brothers, Christ, Luke, Jake and I decided to take broom sticks to see how far we could hit stones. I found what I thought was the perfect stone. I told my brothers, "watch this one fly". I hit that stone harder than ever. My brother Luke happened to be too close to me, and the stick hit him in the face right above the eye. Blood was running down his face, we were so scared that we totally forgot to see how far the stone flew. I got a whipping just the same, as father always told us that we were never to throw or hit stones.

Us four brothers always had great ideas, we were very active and creative. We had too much free time on our hands for our own good, and not enough work. We made most of our toy cars, trucks and tractors from pieces of wood, and a few nails we pulled out of the old barn. We cut a tree limb into short pieces to make the wheels.

SCHOOL DAYS

We had to walk over a mile to Metzler's school. It was an eight grade one room school house with a total of twenty-eight to thirty-six students.

Metzler's School I attended for 6 years

School was not a great experience for my brothers, sisters, and I. We were made fun of in school continually. Even the poor people called us poor. I remember wearing a pair of pants with elastic at the knees. Long black stockings from above the knees down. I was the only one that I ever knew of that wore that type of pant. All of us boys wore hand me down pants with patches on the knees or wherever we made holes in them. Sometimes my mother put patch upon patch, as our clothes had to last all year. No one else had to wear torn and patched pants for school, so you can imagine the ridiculing we received. While the other student's parents were mostly farmers, they had money to live a better life. We were still living without electricity in our home. We were still affected by the Great Depression. Having a large family did not help our situation.

One day my brother Christ accidently got cut deep into the knee with an ax. He was not able to walk to school. After a few weeks my mother thought of a plan for us siblings to pull him in the little wagon to school. One day after his knee was healed, he decided he did not want to go to school. My oldest sister was ordered by our mother to make him go. My sister followed him to the school grounds with a whip in her hand. He never tried to skip school after that.

I remember our teacher was not very nice to us. When my brother Christ was in first grade the teacher got mad at him about something. The teacher walked to Christ's desk and busted a big thick yard stick on his desk. He said to Christ, "I feel like taking you down to the cemetery and burying you alive." Another time the teacher said to the classroom in frustration, "I feel like cutting my head off and throwing it out on the street." I hope and pray that he had the chance to repent to God before he died.

SUMMERS AT MY UNCLE'S FARM

During summer vacation I would go to my uncle Christ's farm, working for money to buy my school clothes and food. I remember when I was there, I fell and broke my left arm halfway between my elbow and my wrist, what excruciating pain. The doctor pulled on my hand, and my uncle held on to my elbow to set it back in place, with no medication to ease the pain. I had a plaster cast on my arm for four weeks. When they removed the cast, the skin was stuck to it and came off along with it. It took a while, but it healed okay.

I had to work hard all summer. I had to drive the horses to plant tobacco, and I had to help hoe the weeds in the fields, a never-ending job. When it came black berry picking time, it was my job to take the berries from farm to farm to sell them pulling a little wagon by hand. I used to get so, tired I could barely go anymore.

I really did enjoy working for my uncle. He made his own cigars from the tobacco he raised, I remember one day he offered me a cigar. He rolled one up for me, and I thought finally I can be a real man. I smoked half of it and felt so cool. I thought I would save the other half for the next day. However, the next day when I lit up again, I got dizzy. My uncle put it out for me and threw it away. I don't know if he wanted to teach me a lesson or what, but he did. I did not know that when you light up a cigar the second time, it is twice as strong. I never tried to smoke again until I was a real man at eighteen years old. Thank God I never liked it.

When summer time was over, my uncle always took me home to get ready to go back to school. I remember him driving me home in an old model T Ford Coupe, I thought was a pretty awesome car, and I felt cool riding in it.

My uncle always came to visit us on Halloween evening. My older brothers decided to pull a trick on him. They blocked up one of his rear wheels of his car a little off the ground. He started it up, put it in gear, turned the hand throttle lever and sped up the motor and it would not move. He tried it again thought he might not have put it in gear correctly. He sped it up again and it still did not move. He got so mad, and when he gets mad he cannot talk, just stutter. He got out stuttering and spitting and looked to see why his car did not move, he didn't see anything wrong and got back in the car and sped up the motor again. As he did that, my brothers pushed the car off the block as he spun the tires and took off. My brothers also tied a string of tin cans behind his car like we do for newlyweds. We could hear him a long-ways off, dragging those cans behind him. He could only drive that old car about fifteen or twenty miles an hour in those days. He enjoyed pulling jokes on others, but he was not a good sport in receiving them.

Us four boys: Back row is Christ, Me, Emma, & Lydia
Front row, Jacob, Mary, & Luke

FUN DAYS

I remember sledding in the snow down a steep hill in our neighbor's meadow on an old piece of tin roof. We went flying down the hill, it was much better than a sled. Eight or ten people could ride at one time. Wow was that ever fun, those were the good old days. Ha! Ha! But, then you had to climb up the hill for another ride, but it was well worth it.

One day my older brothers turned old car tires inside out. This made the tires wide enough for us younger boys to sit inside. We would roll down a steep hill, spinning around inside the tire going so fast it made you dizzy. At times the tire didn't go where it was supposed and hit a tree on the way down. With the tire bent out on the sides, it cushioned us, and we were never hurt much, just little bumps and bruises here and there. We were having so much fun it did not matter.

My father gave me the responsibility to weed approximately half an acre of garden. I had to cultivate all this before I went to my uncle's farm for the summer. I had to push a small hand cultivator with five small prongs, about six inches wide through this whole big garden. This was hard work. One day I got a brilliant idea. My father had what they called a shovel harrow or cultivator pulled by one horse, it was much larger and covered more ground. I called on my three younger brothers to help me. I copied the setup from the horses when they hitched them together to pull a bigger load. I made what they called a triple tree, next a double tree, and then three single trees. I adjusted them accordingly so that each of us would pull equal loads. Now we needed three harnesses, so we could pull this big cultivator. We found some horse halters and used them for harnesses. We put them on our bodies like you put a harness on a horse. Wow, what a great idea. However, I was disappointed when my little brothers could not pull their share of the weight. I pulled two thirds of the load and my two younger brothers together pulled one third of the load. My brother Christ was bigger than the other two, so he was pushing from the back as well as keeping it balanced. As a team, we completed the cultivating in just a short time. When father came home from work that evening, he couldn't believe what he saw. He asked how I did all that in one day? I showed him what we had made working together. I told him that I came up with the idea. He just shook his head and walked away in amazement.

One day us four brothers were walking in our landlord's meadow. The cows had not been grazing there for a while. We saw a salt block that the cows used to lick. We decided to lick it. If it is good for the cows, it must be good for us. We soon learned that salt is good but not too much at one time. We lost all our lunch that was still in our stomachs. Let's just say, we never tried that again.

Us four brothers decided to have a pig rodeo. We had three half grown pigs that our father was raising for meat for the family. We got on the pig's back, boy did we have an exciting ride. The pig's jumped and we went flying. We all tried to stay on the pig's back as long as we could. Eventually, the pig's got tired, while someone was on the pig's back, someone else hit the pig on the backside with a board to get them moving again. The rodeo lasted quite a while longer. We had so much fun until our oldest sister Anna Mae came looking for us. Usually if none of us boys were where she could see us, she had an idea that we were in some kind of mischief. I believe I got on the pig's back and said, "hit it again" just as Anna Mae came around the corner and said, "how would you like to be hit with that board on your backside?" The rodeo ended abruptly. That evening when father came home, we all got a good whipping, I mean he knew how to make it hurt. No sparing the rod and spoiling the child here. Don't tell anyone, but I felt the rodeo was well worth the punishment.

CHAPTER 3
MOST INFLUENTIAL YEARS OF MY YOUTH

HIRED HAND

Come April 16, 1943 on my 14th birthday, I no longer went to school. It was customary for a child to only go to school through 8th grade. My parents needed some extra income to help raise the family. Immediately I was hired out on a farm near Myerstown, PA working for an Amish farmer for thirty dollars a month. He had another hired man that continually made fun of me. I was still suffering from nerve problems from the time I was thrown off the horse at eight years old. I was so overwhelmed and contemplated suicide, but I was too scared to go through with it. Evidently, God still had his hand on me.

When fall came along and the harvesting was completed, the farmer no longer needed two workers, so I was asked to leave. I finished the year with a neighboring farmer, and it was a much better experience.

That following spring of 1943, I came to work on my brother's farm. A real dear man purchased a one hundred seventy-four-acre farm for him. Traditionally, if someone worked on one of his farms, he would purchase their first farm for them, giving them a good start on their own farm. They could pay him back as the farm produced income.

We worked very hard farming with one John Deere A tractor and three horses. The ground on that farm was one of the poorest in the neighborhood. Within three years, it became one of the richest soils on any farm in the area. We had better crops because of all the hard work we put into it, as well as all the compost (manure) we hauled out of the barn. We fed one hundred twenty head of cattle every winter, which added up to a lot of compost hauling. We hauled the hay in from the field loose, not baled like today, and we picked all the corn by hand.

When I was 15 years of age, I was living what I thought to be a normal life. Wheat harvest came along. My brother still didn't have a lot of equipment. So, he hired a wheat harvester to come and cut his crop. They agreed to a certain price to cut the wheat heads only. That meant that we still needed to follow the harvester with our mower to cut the straw that we desperately needed for all the cattle we fed in the barn. Over time the mower blades got dull and began to choke up. I began to get frustrated curse and swear violently. I had learned to curse and swear like the best of them. English didn't have enough meaning, so I did most of the swearing in German. I suppose that this went on for twenty to thirty minutes. I tried to bust the tractor, I took a large wrench from the tractor tool box, and I beat the mower with it, then threw it as far as I could. Afterwards, I was angry again because I had to go pick up the wrench. Finally, my brother came with a sharpened blade, and ended the temper tantrum.

The next day it rained, no harvesting in the rain. My brother decided to do some repairs in the barn. He found an oak plank, almost as hard as nails. He tried to hammer nails into the board, but they would only get stuck, or flew away. He started another nail, pulled the hatchet, back behind his head as far as he could reach, and began to curse. I later counted thirty-two nails in the board, this didn't include the ones that flew away. This went on for quite a while. I suddenly realized I was looking in a mirror, I remembered how I was acting just like that the day before, I suddenly felt very ashamed of myself.

MY CONVERSION

The spirit of God began to deal with me, I saw my ugly reflection in a mirror and I began to talk to God. I said, "Dear God is there anything that I can do to live better, I told God I was sorry for the way I acted the day before, as well as all of my past mistakes." I asked God to forgive me for my actions, I knew offended him.

Customarily, we went to church every other week as we shared the church building with another group of Conservative Mennonites. Several Sundays later I attended church and the minister gave an invitation to come to the Minister's room if you wanted to become a church member. The Lord was dealing with me, and I knew that is what I needed to do, but I was shy and nervous to go by myself.

As Jesus said in *John 3:7 Marvel not that I said unto thee, Ye must be born again.*

And in, **John 3:3 Jesus answered and said unto him, Verily, verily, I say unto thee, <u>except a man be born again, he cannot see the kingdom of God.</u>**

And in *1 John 5:13 These things have I written unto you that believe on the name of the Son of God; <u>that ye may know that ye have eternal life</u>, and that ye may believe on the name of the Son of God.*

My parents decided to visit one of my other brothers that also was a farmer. One of my second cousins was working for him at the time, and that day we became very good friends. We decided we would go together to the Minister's room the next Sunday to become church members.

Sunday came, and I asked my parents to take me to church early, as I wanted to become a church member. My mother said, "if you are sure that is what you want to do, we will go early." We arrived at the church, no one else was there except my cousin. When it came time to enter the pastor's room, no one else showed up. My cousin was shy and did not want to go in if no one else was going. At that point, I had to decide what I was going to do? I felt comfortable with one other person going in with me, but I did not want to go in alone. I felt the Lord tugging at my heart and decided to go in even if I had to do it alone. After I made that decision fifteen other young people showed up including my cousin.

I believe God tested me that day to see if I really meant business. I did not understand it all, but I knew it was right. I believe that is when I really accepted Jesus into my heart. From that day forth I was a changed young man. I had very little understanding about salvation. Even the animals knew when I got saved. The cow switching me in the face with her tail while I was milking no longer irritated me. I didn't kick the cats anymore when they got in my way, and I didn't swear anymore, my life was totally different. Sometimes I still struggled with my anger issues, but I would remember what Jesus had done for me. I would say, "Satan I rebuke you in the name of Jesus, go and bother me no more, I am forgiven, Jesus set me free. I no longer have room for the things of the past."

I had little to no spiritual help or guidance from anyone. I still heard swearing nearly every day. My brother and the other hired man always made fun of me and tried to get me to drink with them, they could not understand the new me. A man we worked with filling silo during harvest time, insisted I go and buy some beer for all of us. The weather was very hot, and we were so thirsty, I gave in to the pressure. When I arrived, the bar tender asked to see my driver's license, I told him I left it at home which was true. He looked at me and said, "I don't believe that you are twenty-one". I never made a very good liar, I was only seventeen years old, so I left. I returned to the farm and told the guys the story. I had a hard time convincing them that I wasn't lying. I never again went to buy beer for anyone.

CHAPTER 4
MY LIFETIME COMPANION

PUPPY LOVE

The third year working with my brother on the farm, I went with him to a place called the Green Dragon, a local farmer's market and small animal and cattle auction. It was on Friday December 19. 1947, I was now eighteen years old. As I was walking around the market with a group of Mennonite boys, I saw this beautiful Amish girl, it was love at first sight. It was a very cold evening and somehow her father allowed her to wear a beautiful black leather jacket, pretty fancy and not a church approved attire for an Amish girl. At the top opening of her jacket was a small puppy. It was her favorite puppy that her and her father brought to sell at the auction, she did not want to let it go.

I saw her again in one of the other buildings. The group of Mennonite boys that I was with stopped close to the group of Mennonite and Amish girls to check them out. I just couldn't take my eyes off this beautiful Amish girl that I had seen earlier with the puppy. I wanted to date her with all my heart. Something was totally different about her.

My second cousin was with us and said he had to go home, I anxiously walked with him to the cable bridge where he had to cross the creek. I asked him, "Why don't you let me ask that Amish girl for a date for you?" He replied, "I am not interested". I insisted, and he looked at me and said, "Maybe you want me to ask her for you." I squirmed a bit and said, "Well ok!" He had no idea how bad I wanted to date her. Asking a girl for your friend, was customary among our group of Mennonites. By now you probably believe me when I say that I was an extremely shy person. We went back to the building where the girls were. I was so excited and hoping she was still there, and she was. My second cousin walked right up to her and introduced himself and said, "There is a young man over there that would like to ask you for a date." She looked our way and said, "which one is it?" He called me out and told me to turn around, I was totally embarrassed. I turned around and she saw my blushing face. I saw her nod her head "yes".

Now the real embarrassment came, in front of all those young people I had to go talk to her and introduce myself and ask her for her name, she replied, "Anna Zook". She agreed to go out with me, so we decided to meet on Saturday night in New Holland on the corner of Kauffman's Hardware Store. I could not pick her up at her home because her father would not approve of his young daughter dating anyone outside of the Amish faith. We had a date that night and again on Sunday night. We double dated with my cousin and his girlfriend. We had a wonderful time together.

The following week was Christmas. On Sunday evening at the end of our date, we were saying our goodbyes. I told Anna, I thought we should break up. I was honest and explained that I don't have any money to buy her a Christmas present. I was ashamed, but she made me feel like she understood. She replied, I don't have any money for a Christmas present either. Quickly I saw the opportunity and took it. I asked her if she wanted to go out next Saturday evening, immediately she replied "YES". That was the beginning of a marvelous, miraculous beautiful relationship between us for life.

In August 1948, I saw my love, my sweet heart abused in a family quarrel. I told her that she did not need to take this abuse. I asked her to marry me and let me take care of her. I told her that I loved her and that she cannot continue to live like this. She agreed, and we decided to get married as soon as possible. We set the wedding date for September

25, 1948. We went to the preacher and told him about our wedding plans and asked him to officiate. We were hoping for some council and advice. When we left his house, we were disappointed. The only advice he gave was that we would have some problems, but the Lord would help us work them out.

When the wedding day arrived, the preacher showed up at the house early. Again, we were hoping to receive some council, He only asked us about the details, and our plans. He replied, "May God bless you!"

OUR LIFE JOURNEY BEGINS

We started our new life together. Things were not easy. Several months after the wedding, a friend of ours borrowed our car and forgot to cover the radiator with a big blanket, I had in the car for that purpose. We lost our car when the engine froze up because the antifreeze was low. He never paid us for the damages, it was a complete loss.

We bought another car that turned out to be a lemon. We struggled financially for a while. As you may well remember that Satan always gave me double the trouble in almost everything. We couldn't make it financially, so we moved in with Anna's parents the rest of the winter. We soon had enough money saved to get a better car, a 1937 Ford in excellent condition.

Our spiritual walk together began. We joined a more spiritual Mennonite Church called the Lancaster Conference Mennonites. Together we decided to serve the Lord there. I was no longer old order Mennonite and Anna was no longer Amish. This group of Mennonites believed in revival meetings, Sunday School as well as summer Bible School. We were blessed to be a part of a church that you could feel the presence of God in the services and they encouraged spiritual growth.

Moving from place to place as I had experienced from childhood continued with my young bride. We were ready to experience our own adventures. We soon moved out of Anna's parent's home, to our first job on a farm near East Petersburg, PA. I was to manage a small farm for a business man. God began to bless us. Our first son Melvin Jr was born that summer. But things didn't work out very well on this farm, it was time to move on.

We moved onto a dairy farm near Manheim, PA. Our son Mervin was born there. We lived and worked there several years until the landlord's son got married. Since he needed the house for his new bride, we needed to find another place.

We moved on a farm near Mount Joy, PA. We were not there long when we were offered a much better deal to work and live on a farm near Rohrerstown, PA.

I fed cattle and pigs in the barn for the farmer as well as worked for him on a second farm. We had good relations with him, and he allowed me to raise tobacco as part of my wages. In the winter after the tobacco was sold, I worked in the City of Lancaster for a Moving Van Company. It was a blessing to work there, I was able to make extra money that was really needed for the family. During the years we lived there, God added 3 more children to our family. The farmer I worked for had twin sons that graduated from high school. He then had all the labor he needed, and I was out of another job. He allowed us to continue to live there for several more years, feeding his cattle for the rent. I started a job working at the Trojan Boat Factory. Sometime later, the farmer sold the farm we were living on and we had to move on.

CHAPTER 5
CAREER CHANGE

STARTING MY OWN BUSINESS

We moved to Mascot, PA, renting a house while still working at the Trojan Boat Factory. Several years later, the factory discontinued one of their small boat models. I decided to buy the wooden forms and patterns and start making the boats myself. An Amish man that I worked with had furniture building equipment in his barn to help get us started. We continued to work at the boat factory during the day and made our own boats at night.

I purchased the wood and additional tools to make our first boat. By the time the boat was nearly finished, I was able to buy more lumber and paint for two more boats. When the first boat was finished, she was a beauty, we were so proud.

A farmer came by one day. He told us that he believes he could sell our boats. We decided to let him take our beautiful boat for two weeks to different boat dealers to see what he could do. He came back with a big surprise. He told us these boats sell like hot cakes and that we will not be able to supply the amount of boats needed working part time in this barn alone. He told us that his brother is an implement dealer and has some room to spare where we can do the painting, once the boats are built. We were now full time in the boat business.

About a week later the farmer came back with more orders. He told us that he and his brother would both like to invest $20,000.00 to start a boat factory and partner with us.

Now we had a problem, three partners are too many, and four is out of the question. The business was in my friend's barn, guess who was bumped out – me. They agreed to pay me for my time I had recorded as well as all the tools I had purchased. I said "no". My friend said, "you have no choice, take it or leave it". They agreed to hire me at a fair price and it was more than I was able to earn at the Trojan Boat Factory, so I accepted.

I was the one with all the knowledge and ability to do everything from start to finish. They knew they could not do it without me. I knew how to make patterns for new models, how to run and set up every machine in the shop, how to run the paint shop and do all the painting. I was their key man.

Later they built another building and hired more men. I was made foreman of the woodworking shop as well as the assembly plant.

They decided to make a larger boat. The Amish man needed me to help in the development. We worked hard to get it into production. When we completed it, one of the owners took it to the dealers. Immediately they got orders more than we were able to build. The owners offered a very good bonus if we can build a certain amount of boats by a set date. The other foreman was a very close friend to the owners. He asked them to let him be foreman over the whole plant. They demoted me and put me back in the paint department, painting parts.

Later they needed a final inspector to make sure the boats were ready for shipping. I was the most qualified man for the job. The dead line for the boats was getting close. We were somewhat behind, when I discovered some defects and rejected a boat. The foreman was furious and reprimanded me in front of the other employees. The next time I didn't reject the boat for the same defects, he screamed at me again. He began to make it very difficult for me. He was worried about his big bonus he was expecting to get if he finished before the deadline and he was getting very frustrated. I could not take any more of his abuse and I turned to him and told him to find someone else for the job, I was turning in my two-week resignation. He told me if I wanted to do that, I could leave right now, so, I did.

I was upset, the company was stolen from me. God had given me the gift to start the boat building. It was my money that started it and now it was all gone. Did I file a law suit? No, I never even thought about it. You see God repays when you mistreat others, it comes home every time. Several years after I quit, the boat company went bankrupt.

I know God was shaping and preparing me for the future. Sometimes we do not understand everything and most times, it is best if we don't. He was preparing me for something much greater than boat building later in life, Praise God. He was working out his plan in my life, not mine. Sometimes our disappointments are God's appointments.

CHAPTER 6
MOLDING ME AND MAKING ME

AN EXPERIENCE THAT CHANGED
MY LIFE FOREVER

The boat experience set me back a few steps. During this time the Lord began to deal with my heart. I began searching for the deeper things of God. I knew that there was more to life than just working and being a good Christian. I was doing my best to follow Him. I started searching for more of God, and asked him if this was all he had for me?

Our pastor announced the following Sunday he was going to preach on divine healing. I knew that the Mennonites always said that healing was not for today, it was for the time of the Apostles as they did not have the New Testament, so I was intrigued. That Sunday, Anna was not able to go along to church. I entered the church alone, a bit late. The congregation was praying when I started to enter. I stood there in the hallway not able to move. When the usher walked in, he looked at me and asked if I was alright, I told him that I am sure I will be alright. He said that I better go lay down. I assured him again that I would be ok. He said again, you better go see a doctor you do not look good. I assured him one more time that I would be ok. He insisted that someone take me to the doctor. I do not know what he saw, I only knew the pain I was feeling was unlike anything I ever experienced, I thought I was dying. I knew I was in trouble. My Sunday School Teacher volunteered to take me. He did not know where to find a Doctor on a

Sunday morning, so he took me to the hospital. Later I was told that my face was white as a sheet.

When they took me through the hospital door, God spoke to me and said, "You failed me!" I said, "Dear God, how, I am dying." He said, "I wanted to do a miracle in the Mennonite Church this morning". I replied, "Dear God, if you heal me this morning I will do my best to never fail you again, so please help me God."

A nurse kept checking on me until a doctor came. It was unbelievable that in the largest hospital in Lancaster, PA they could not locate a doctor for three and a half hours. You see, again God had a plan bigger than ours. He wanted to prove to me that he was in control. I did not know how to respond to God. I was in the very beginning process of understanding God in the miraculous. By the time they located a doctor, I was totally healed. The doctor said, you must have had some severe indigestion that went away. I knew for sure God had healed me.

I went back to the church and began to ask how I can have more of God. Our Sunday School Teacher replied, "Melvin, it is the Baptism of the Holy Spirit." I said, "Brother, I got it all when I got saved." He replied, "Melvin, I know you don't understand, just don't be afraid. I know you heard a lot of negative things about the Holy Spirit, this is the way that the Devil tries to keep many people from receiving all God has for them." That day my teacher prayed for me to receive the Holy Spirit. I didn't receive it right then, I went home to my bed room to pray. I was determined to receive everything that God had for me. I said, "Dear Lord if this is still for today please help me to receive it. Forgive me for all my doubts and fears, as well as all the negative things I have said and have been taught." As I prayed this short prayer, suddenly, I was able to receive the Baptism of the Holy Spirit with the evidence of speaking in tongues.

I can now see that I was never taught correctly about the baptism of the Holy Spirit in the Mennonite Church. We were taught that the Spiritual Gifts were only for the Early Church, as they did not have the New Testament. They would use the following scripture to try and prove their point:

1 Corinthians 13:8 ¶ Charity never faileth: but whether there be prophecies, they shall fail; whether there be tongues, they shall cease; whether there be knowledge, it shall vanish away.

9 For we know in part, and we prophesy in part.

10 But when that which is perfect is come, then that which is in part shall be done away.

11 When I was a child, I spake as a child, I understood as a child, I thought as a child: but when I became a man, I put away childish things.

12 For now we see through a glass, darkly; but then face to face: now I know in part; but then shall I know even as also I am known.

13 And now abideth faith, hope, charity, these three; but the greatest of these is charity.

We were taught that the perfect had come, the New Testament. So, we no longer needed these gifts. You see in *verse 8 it says, whether there are prophecies, they will fail; whether there are tongues, they will cease; whether there is knowledge, it will vanish away.* You see that knowledge is included in this group. I am sure that you must agree with me that knowledge has not vanished away. Sometimes we pick out parts of the scriptures that suits our belief instead of taking them in context as they are written in the Bible. Speaking in tongues to the religious Church was considered as speaking as a child since you do not understand.

The scriptures say in,

> *Romans 8:26* ¶ <u>*Likewise the Spirit also helpeth our*</u> <u>*infirmities: for we know not what we should pray for*</u> <u>*as we ought: but the Spirit itself maketh intercession*</u> <u>*for us with groanings which cannot be uttered.*</u>
>
> *27 And he that searcheth the hearts knoweth what is the mind of the Spirit, because he maketh intercession for the saints according to the will of God.*
>
> *28 And we know that all things work together for good to them that love God, to them who are the called according to his purpose.*

After I received the gift of the Holy Spirit, I began to rejoice and thank God. A week later, still searching for more of God, I felt God telling me to go to a Pentecostal Church in Lancaster, PA. In the service the leader said let us pray, and everyone prayed at the same time. Again, I was totally confused. I said dear God, how in the world could you hear all these prayers at the same time. I was used to only one person praying at a time in church, we were taught that this was the only way to pray. I never stopped to think that when we prayed at mealtime at home, everyone prayed silent prayers, and that was more than one person praying at a time. Many times, with our religion we put our great big God in a tiny little box in our minds. But I freaked out, it was too much to handle. I said, "Dear God if you get me out of this place, my shadow will not darken the door step of this church again." It did open my eyes to the fact that if God could not hear one hundred-fifty to one hundred-seventy-five people praying at the same time, how in the world could he hear all the prayers of all his people around the world.

Two weeks later I was swallowing my pride and went back to church. While I was there, God spoke to me to work with the brother in Tower City, PA. I left the church that night knowing that God had spoken again. I was not taught this, it was not the Mennonite way. God also told me that I would soon be taking over the Ministry. I was willing to go help but take over the work someone else started was another thing. God said don't worry about the details. I was not rebellious, only scared.

It was not long when it happened just as God had spoken. The pastor said, I need to spend some time with my family, I am turning the work over to you. I said "no, I will help you, but not lead." I felt I was not ready. His reply was, "from now on the work is in your hands." Little did I know that God was preparing me for the Mission Field later.

I felt led to visit that same Pentecostal Church in Lancaster City again. Suddenly during the worship, my chin began to vibrate seemingly uncontrollable. I got scared and said, "Devil I rebuke you, stop it now in the name of Jesus." To my surprise it stopped. Again, I was really scared. I really wanted to be sure if this was from God, or from the Devil. Now I was in a pickle, what do I do? I said, "Dear God, if this really was from you, then please forgive me and let it start again." Immediately it started again. God does not get offended like we do sometimes. He knows how ignorant we are. I finally learned how to surrender to the Holy Spirit. I gave a message in tongues. Afterwards I gave the interpretation. Someone told me later that they had a vision of Jesus standing behind me during that time. I needed that confirmation, I still had a lot of fear because of my former teaching that tongues, was of the devil.

I will never forget an experience I had in a church when a demon possessed person spoke in tongues. It was the scariest experience I ever had in my life. Immediately God helped me to know that it was from the devil. There was no question. I found out the devil has a counterfeit to deceive the weak Christians, the doubters, unbelievers and those taught against tongues in many church denominations. Let me tell you, tongues are real. You see that there cannot be a counterfeit, without first being real.

Romans 8:26 ¶ Likewise the Spirit also helpeth our infirmities: for we know not what we should pray for as we ought: but the Spirit itself maketh intercession for us with <u>groanings which cannot be uttered</u>.

27 And he that searcheth the hearts knoweth what is the mind of the Spirit, <u>because he maketh intercession for the saints according to the will of God.</u>

Jude 1:20 But ye, beloved, building up yourselves on your most holy faith, praying in the Holy Ghost,

Ephesians 6:8 praying always with all prayer and supplication in the Spirit, being watchful to this end with all perseverance and supplication for all the saints—

Acts 1:4 And, being assembled together with them, <u>commanded them</u> that they should not depart from Jerusalem, but wait for the promise of the Father, which, saith he, ye have heard of me.

5 For John truly baptized with water; but ye shall be baptized with the <u>Holy Ghost</u> not many days hence.

You can see that the Baptism of the Holy Spirit is one of the most powerful tools in the Christian's life and Ministry. For this cause the enemy of our soul brings more confusion in the body of Christ than any other subject. If he can confuse the believers on this subject, then he keeps the body of Christ powerless.

TESTING, GROWING, AND PREPARING

When the Lord is moving, the devil always does his best to hinder the working of God in your life. I have learned that if Satan isn't fighting you, you are not doing something right. While I was pastoring the church in Tower City we moved the congregation to Wiconisco. Our congregation had now moved from a storefront, to a church building. The church went through many trials, the devil tried his best to discourage me and cause me to give up the ministry.

One evening I came home after a beautiful time of ministering at the church, Anna told me that someone had visited her while I was gone. Asking her "what is wrong with Melvin? He is no longer a Mennonite, and he should know better. He is not a Christian if he is not in the Mennonite faith, and he cannot go to heaven. "Anna was not aware that the people that came to visit her while I was preaching, were mostly hindering the call of God in my life as well as our personal relationship.

I came home from church on another occasion and Anna was very upset, she again had visitors that day. Satan uses well-meaning people to put suggestions in your mind. She began to accuse me of things, saying, "I know why you are hauling those widows to your church, I know it all." She accused me of every sin in the Bible. For some reason, I had peace in my heart, I didn't even try to vindicate myself, I just listened.

She ran to the bedroom and threw herself onto the bed. I followed her as we were both crying and laid on the bed beside her. I knew that there was no way to make her believe that I did nothing wrong, I knew that God knew my thoughts and actions were pure and innocent and He had it all under control. I put my arm around Anna and said, "Honey will you please forgive me." She replied, "Sure." When one companion can keep the victory, somehow both can have a glorious outcome. Before I was a Christian, I didn't always have this gift and would have lost my temper.

After this she started going with me to church or wherever I was preaching. The devil was trying his best to discourage me and cause me to quit trusting God and preaching the gospel, he knew God had a plan for me.

GOD SPARED MY LIFE AGAIN

When I left the boat factory, I started driving tractor trailer for a Propane Distributor, as well as pastoring the church. One of my co-worker's vehicle broke down and asked me to assist him. I knew I was too sleepy to drive, but I decided to go and help him anyway. I was driving up the Gap Hill. When I was near the top I fell asleep driving 55 miles an hour. There was a tractor trailer going up the hill in front of me at about 5 miles an hour. I woke up just seconds before I ran into the back of him. I jerked the wheel to the left to miss him, but it was too late I hit him. I was about half a car width when hitting the back of his truck, causing the back end of the car to spin around into the oncoming lane and sat there sideways blocking the road. I knew I was a sitting duck and I had to get out of the car. The car door was jammed partially open from the collision. I could not open it any further but decided to try and squeeze out. I wiggled my way through the opening and was stuck as a car came over the crest of the hill right toward me. I could not climb back into the car or get out to avoid being crushed, I was trapped, I could just hope and pray that the driver saw me and had enough time to get stopped. I stood there frozen thinking that was it, I was not going to make it. To my surprise, the car was able to come to a complete stop before hitting me. After the accident, my friend came to pick me up and we stopped at the Black Horse Restaurant to eat. A couple came into the restaurant while we were there talking about the bad accident on the Gap Hill and they were very sure that no one came out of that accident alive. I looked at them and said, I was the driver of that car. They looked at me in amazement and asked how I was able to get out of that car alive and be able to walk in here to eat. I told them that only God knows.

I got off the road and began to do auto repair in a vacant building close to our home. I made a deal with the owner, he would get half the profit to cover the rent. This was ok in the beginning, but God began to bless my business. The farmers and neighbors told their friends about the excellent mechanic work at a really good price. The work started to come in, in abundance. I had to buy the supplies, parts and tools for the shop out of my half of the profit, it was not working for me, I was doing all the work and the landlord was making all the profit. The landlord was not willing to change the deal we had made.

The following morning, I saw a "For Lease" sign on a gas station with two bays and an apartment upstairs over the garage for my family. It had been for sale for eighteen years, and nobody bought it, so I decided to lease it. It was perfect for me and my family. We lived in the small upstairs apartment with 8 children and I could walk to work. God again blessed my work and efforts. Soon I had all the work I could handle and more and I hired two part time workers.

One day, a man came along and said to me, you have a perfect place here to sell cars. He said he would buy the cars and I could repair them. When we sell the cars, I would get reimbursed for the cost of the parts and we would split the profit. What a blessing, it was a great plan. We sold the cars to the customer on credit, one half down with no credit check. Business increased abundantly.

We were in the garage only one year and six months when a man was driving past and saw the great business we had, and he purchased the garage out from under us. Now what do we do? We had to move on.

My partner in auto sales told me, that I was working way too much and too hard. He suggested that we lease a car lot, then I would only have to work on our cars. That sounded great to me. I leased a corner lot near Morgantown, PA. About six months later, my partner came to me and said, "I am going to run the car business by myself." I replied, "You cannot do that, I have the lease on the property in my name and that is final." He said, "No, I went into your filing cabinet, tore up your lease and had another one drawn in my name." Once again, I was facing defeat, rejection and the humiliation of losing a business.

You may ask why did I get dumped out of business so many times? Why did I not file a law suit? God always blessed me when I let him run my business. But, God had a plan for me, bigger than I could ever imagine, beyond my understanding, and far above that which I can ask or think. Once again, God was trying to prepare me and shape me, letting me know that he was in control of my future. When one door closes, another opens.

A NEW ADVENTURE

That same afternoon I lost the car lot lease, a potato and tomato farmer from Elverson, PA came by and told me he had an emergency and needed a truck driver now. His driver walked off and left him. The truck was loaded with tomatoes and the packing plant in New Jersey closes at midnight. He said he knew that at one time I drove a smaller truck for his uncle, and he believes I could drive his tractor-trailer. He pleaded with me for my help. I told him that I would do it and I made the delivery before closing.

The next day the farmer came to me and asked me to drive his truck regularly. I committed to drive locally, at that time, I was still pastoring the church in Wiconisco, PA. As time went on, I made other trips for him from Maine to South Carolina.

One day I made a trip to Florida to bring back a load of citrus fruit for salad. On my return trip I was traveling around fifty-five miles per hour when suddenly I saw a sign that read "Gross Load Limit 6 Tons", I was hauling a gross weight load of 31 tons. I was going too fast to stop, I could only step on the gas. The last part of the bridge I noticed was planked boards. I did not know what else to do but to pray in the name of Jesus. Somehow, I ended up on the other side, only God knows how I made it. The devil missed again.

One day I came back from a trip and the boss man asked me if I could possibly deliver a load of Pillsbury frozen cakes to Midland Texas. From there I needed to go to Pharr, TX to pick up a load of fruit for my back haul. I was able to have another minister take my place at church for me that Sunday, so I agreed to take the trip.

I arrived in Pharr, TX late on Saturday night. On Sunday morning I overslept and missed the Sunday morning service in the local Assembly of God Church, so I attended the evening service. I was introduced to two missionaries. The one invited me to go with him to Mexico the next afternoon. I told him that I was scheduled to pick up a load of fruit the next morning to head back to PA, but if it didn't work out I would meet him at the church.

On Monday morning the broker told me that since I had a refrigerated truck he could get a load of vegetables for me, which pays double the price of fruit, but I could not load up until Tuesday morning. God worked it out that I could take the trip to Mexico, so I hurried to the church to meet the missionary.

The missionary showed up and I went with him to Mexico to a church service. Arriving at the village in Mexico, we were asked to pray for a lady that was sick in bed, all doubled up with pain. We went to her home and prayed for her, and I saw my first great miracle. After prayer the lady jumped up in the bed. She started praising the Lord and led the way on foot to the service where I witnessed even more miracles that evening.

When we returned to the church in Pharr, TX. I was tremendously overwhelmed. I never saw God moving in this manner. The missionary asked me to go with him again the next day. I told him that the broker had promised a load for the following day, but if something comes up again, I would meet him at the church. I checked in with the broker around noon the next day, and he said he could not finish the load and needed another day. I again hurried to the church and met the missionary.

We loaded the van with tracts and off we went. We met a family in Reynosa, MX, and we headed out into the countryside. We threw tracts out the window to the villagers as we drove by. We had to be very careful, sometimes the children would run out into the street, almost in front of the vehicle because they wanted the tracts so badly. I was so amazed by their hunger for the Word of God.

The missionary told me we were stopping at a village on the way to the church service. We were going to sing and give our testimonies, hoping the people there will ask us to come back to preach. They had visited there before, and the people of the village were not very receptive. I did not know the Spanish language, so I could not participate. They sang songs, and some testified and sang more songs. The missionary asked me to testify. I began to testify in English and the missionary interpreted into Spanish. I began telling them how good Jesus has been to me, and what he has done in my life. I was so touched by the presence of God.

When I finished, a man seemingly dressed better than the rest called the Missionary over to him. The missionary told me after we left that the well-dressed man was the village Judge. He told me the Judge invited us to come to their village to preach any time. He said, "This is my house, it is available to you." I was so blessed to think that my testimony may have been part of the reason the door was opened as they had visited there before, and nothing had happened. We drove several more miles, you could only see a few houses. The service was held in one of them. People started pouring in, not sure where they came from. There were no cars, no transportation, they walked to church. When service time came the house was full and many stood outdoors to hear the gospel. After the song service was over, the missionary announced the preacher from Pennsylvania will bring the message, and he would interpret.

I stepped up next to him and my mind went totally blank. I prayed, "Dear Lord Jesus please give me the words to say. Lord you never let me down before, please help me." I was so humbled at what I was experiencing, I was speechless. I never saw people so hungry for the word of God, I was so overwhelmed, I began to weep like a baby. I quoted *John 3:16*, and the Lord told me to give the altar call. I said, "God I still have not preached". I could not stop crying and gave the altar call as God said. To my surprise, half the congregation came forth weeping. After praying for them they all said they accepted Jesus in their heart. The missionary asked me if I would pray for the sick? Crying, I said "Yes." I gave the call for prayer for the sick, and again, a large part of the congregation came forward. Those on the inside of the house had to make room for those that came in from the outside for prayer. I stood and wept and wept, praying for the sick. Afterwards everyone claimed that they were healed. Again, I was overwhelmed, I never saw anything like this in all my life.

Back to Texas, and back to work. I picked up my load the next day and began the return trip home. I was coming through Arkansas, crossing over a narrow bridge, when I saw another tractor trailer coming toward me with his dual wheels on my side of the yellow line. I knew that there was no humanly possible way we were both going to make it across. I rubbed my wheels, up against the curb and miraculously I got past him without a scratch. Only God knows how. He gave me another miracle. God is so good.

As I was driving and meditating on what the Lord wants me to do with what I learned and experienced in Mexico, I felt led to commit to give God half of the offerings to missions from the church I was pastoring in Wiconisco, PA.

Up until that time, the offerings that came in were no more than around $5.00 to $7.00 a month. They did not cover the utilities or the rent for the church building, which was $30.00, so, it had to come out of my pocket. The first month we sent $3.50 to the missionary. The next month we sent $7.00 and a few cents. The third month we sent $15.00. The fourth month we sent $32.00 and a few cents. I no longer needed to pay the rent on the building, God was blessing us for our giving. You can see what happens when you start supporting missions, God will bless you, and bring the increase. You can never out give God.

One day, coming home from church, I saw a tent meeting in progress. Anna and our son Melvin Jr went with me to the service. Everything went fine until time to dismiss the meeting. The Evangelist started pacing from one end of the platform to the other. Finally, he said, "I must obey God. God is dealing with someone under this tent about Mexico. I don't know whether it is going to Mexico or supporting some Missionary in Mexico. Whoever you are, please come forward." Something seemed to grab me by the seat of my pants, it picked me up from the chair I was sitting on. My feet started taking me forward, I said, "No Lord it is not me, I cannot go. We are already supporting the missionary with half of the offering from the church, NO, it is not me." As I was being pushed forward I looked behind me and Anna was following me. I knew I could never go to the Mission Field. Anna had already told me that I got her out of the Amish Church, but I will never get her out of the Mennonite Church, and that was final. At the alter, different people began to prophesy saying all kind of things that would come to pass when we got to Mexico, I was shocked. They kept on prophesying, I spoke to the Lord in silence. Nobody knew what I said in my spirit, it was between God and I. I said,

"God, if you want us to go to Mexico, there are three things you must do:

#1 You must make my wife willing to go. I will not go without my family, we had 8 children and one on the way. I thought there was no way that would be possible whatsoever.

#2 Lord you must put a pastor in the small church I was pastoring. No one wanted to help pastor the church in the past because the people were extremely poor;

#3. Lord you must supply the finances for the trip.

Answers came in reverse order as follows:

#1 At that very moment the Evangelist looked at me and said, when you are on your way to Mexico, stop in at our church in Washington PA. There will be $100.00 waiting for you when you get there.

#2 One month later the Lord sent a pastor to the church. He promised to take over when we leave.

#3 One month after that, Anna said, if you feel it is the will of God, I am willing to try. Only God can do this.

We did not get much support from anyone. They were very respectful to us in not showing their doubt, but we could tell in their heart they could not believe that God would call a family with 9 children to the Mission Field. People kept asking us where we will live, what will we do, we told them, God will provide and direct our path. Honestly, we did not know, we were stepping out 100% in faith, trusting God all the way. Pastors from the local churches did not support us and thought we were out of our mind. My own brother said if we needed money to come back, he would loan it to us. It felt like everyone thought we were going to fail, and we would be back within a couple of months.

As the Bible story goes, Noah built the ark and told everyone that God told him that a flood was coming, it would rain for forty days, and forty nights. Up to that point it never rained, they did not know what rain was. The people ridiculed Noah. He put his faith in God and obeyed him, so we did also.

Six months later, Saturday, December 29th, between Christmas and the New Year, we were in the car ready to leave for Mexico. We had nine children, $6 dollars in our pocket, a tank full of gas, and all our belongings loaded into an old 1954 Ford Station Wagon that my brother told me, he would not drive to Harrisburg 36 miles away in that thing.

The car we traveled in fully loaded.
From Pennsylvania to Texas – approx. 2000 miles.

While we were saying our last goodbyes to Anna's family we saw a car come flying in the road. It was a family we had met several months prior. They thanked God we were still there. After meeting us and knowing we would be going to the Mission Field with a large family, they sent a letter to some friends in San Juan, Texas (TX) to see what they could do to help. They just got the return letter that morning, and it stated that there is a house waiting for us in San Juan, TX." You see, God is always on time, but it is in his time.

He wanted to remind us in the last minutes, that we were doing the right thing, and he has everything under control. We can trust him with the details, we just had to be willing to go, and we did.

CHAPTER 7
STEPPING OUT IN FAITH

LEAVING FOR MEXICO

We left for Mexico and headed for Washington PA. to meet the Evangelist that told us there would be a $100.00 waiting for us.

On the way we decided to get off the turnpike in Summerset County, PA and visit a family we heard spent some time in Mexico with a missionary friend. We were hoping to get some information and encouragement, instead of being encouraged, they thought there was something wrong with us, like we were out of our minds. We left their house, so discouraged. Anna and I both felt like turning back and giving up.

We returned to the Turnpike entrance to continue our journey, still not sure which way we were going to go. The man at the toll booth asked us, which way we were traveling, and my reply was, *"West, I guess."* He said that was okay and proceeded to tell us that the East bound road is completely snowed shut. West bound lane is the only one open, what a coincidence or was it? God knew our thoughts and knew that we were discouraged, and we needed an extra push to guide us in the right direction, He never left us down in-spite of our unbelief.

When we arrived at the church in Washington, PA, the pastor sent a lady to put us up for the night in the parsonage. The next morning Anna and I with all 9 children sat in the front row in the service. The pastor never acknowledged us sitting there. After the service ended, he came to us in private and said that he was sorry, they had a missionary come through on Thursday and they emptied the treasury completely, they had nothing to give us.

We sat there discouraged again, wondering what to do now, without the one hundred dollars for gas to get us to Texas. The pastor could not believe he made such a big mistake. He felt bad that he prophesied over me to go to Mexico, and he would have on hundred dollars waiting for us for our journey, and he could not keep his promise. He said he wanted to buy some food for us to eat. When he returned with the food, he said, "May God bless you". Still muttering to himself as he walked away. "How could I have made such a big mistake?"

God was really working hard on him and would not let him go. About fifteen minutes later as we were finishing eating, he came back again, opened his wallet and gave me fifty dollars of his personal money, he stated that was all he had. Sometime later, he told us that he thought we stepped out in faith on his prophesy alone and he was afraid that we would fall flat on our faces. God strengthened his faith and revealed to him that if he can take care of two, on the Mission Field, he can take care of eleven.

I remembered my Senior Pastor and Mentor, Rev. Luke Weaver from Grace Chapel in Elizabethtown, PA told me to be sure to stop in at a church in Berlin Ohio where a group of former Amish people got saved and filled with the Holy Spirit and started a new church. Had we received the offering in Washington, PA, we would have had enough money to get to Texas, but God had other plans, he was not finished, and we headed for Ohio.

We had no cell phones in those days, or even a phone number to call the pastor. When we arrived in town, we stopped at the local gas station and asked for directions. The attendant knew the pastor and told us that he was leaving for Florida for the Annual Convention at Gospel Crusade. They thought that we could possibly still catch him at his house.

They gave us the address, and when we arrived at the pastor's home, no one was there.

We sat there a bit trying to figure out what to do, how could we have come this far, and be so wrong. We still did not get the picture. We were not making the decisions, God was. We just had to learn to recognize his voice.

We saw a lady walk across the yard toward us, it was the pastor's mother-in-law. We told her that we were on our way to Mexico to be Missionaries. Rev. Luke Weaver suggested we stop at their church on our way. She told us the pastor just left for Florida to a convention, but she said it would be okay for us to make ourselves at home in the pastor's house. She stated that they just bought a washer and dryer and we would be welcome to use it. She also handed me a twenty-dollar bill and said that maybe this would help a little.

We asked God, what do we do now and where do we go from here? Shortly after she left, one of the elders of the church and his wife showed up. They invited us to go with them to another church for New Year's Eve service, and we accepted.

That evening at the service, there was a lady in a wheel chair. I felt the Lord telling me to pray for her, so she could get up from the wheel chair and walk. A voice inside my head said, "And what if it doesn't happen, you will make a fool of yourself." Being new in the working of the Lord, my faith waivered and I didn't do anything. I found out later that Anna had the same feeling and our fear robbed us from obeying the Lord.

I started seeking God's direction as to where he wanted us to go next. I thought that maybe the Lord wanted us to go to Florida to the Convention where the pastor went, I had credentials with the same Ministerial Fellowship. I prayed to the Lord and asked him to show us which way he wanted us to go. Again, our faith was weakening, and we needed a sign of assurance from God. I put out a fleece before him and said, "Lord if the sun is shining in the morning, we will know that you want us to go west to Texas, but if the snow is falling, we will know that you want us to go to Florida." Well guess what, in the morning the sun was shining, and the snow was falling. Now what, what did this mean? So, we felt we should stay still and wait another day. That evening we went to bed with the same fleece before God, sun or snow, which way to go.

The next morning again, the sun was shining, and the snow was falling. The Lord spoke to us, I will show you the way." We no longer needed to seek for a sign. We understood what God's voice sounded like when he spoke to us.

One of the families from the church invited us to eat an early lunch with them, afterwards we planned on leaving, thinking we needed to get our children to Texas and get them registered for school as soon as possible. After we were finished eating we got talking about different things. Suddenly, I realized it was getting late, it was already two o'clock in the afternoon. The brother's wife asked why we wouldn't just stay another night. She proposed that if I help her husband setup for the service in the new church building, we could call the congregation and arrange a special service that night for us to minister. We agreed, so they called the members of the church and invited them to come out to hear me preach, and we had a beautiful service.

During the worship service, the lady that was playing the piano got so blessed that she fell off the piano bench, but the piano kept right on playing. We were seeing strange things that we did not understand, but when you recall that God could speak to the prophet using a donkey recorded in the Bible in Numbers 22:29-30, you ask no questions. You know, sometimes we are so narrow minded that God finds it is almost impossible to work with us. He is so merciful and longsuffering. At the end of the service, a Sunday School class came into the service. carrying a jug about half full of change and said they have been praying for a Missionary to come so they could donate the money they have collected, and we are the missionaries they want to bless. That evening, the Lord blessed us with a little over three hundred and thirty-two dollars, in 1963 that was a lot of money.

The next morning the sun was shining no snow was falling, so we headed for San Juan, Texas and the Mexican Border. Gasoline was four to five gallons for one dollar, so we had plenty of money to get there. We even had money to stop and buy food for the children. At that time, we could buy ten hamburgers for a dollar, with two dollars we could feed the whole family. God is good!!

The trip was not without its challenges. We had our one wheeled trailer loaded too heavy, that it broke the suspension, we had to stop and get it repaired.

Travelling was slow with nine children and not many roads were super highways in those days. We slept in the car most of the time, cuddled up to stay warm. When we got into Texas, to our surprise it was very warm, in January. Our last night on the road we stopped to sleep in a rest area. The weather was so nice the boys slept outside on the picnic tables. We ate cereal the next morning (11 bowls) and hit the road, "San Juan or bust".

CHAPTER 8
AND SO, IT BEGINS

ARRIVING IN SAN JUAN, TEXAS

On January 7th, 1963, we arrived at the house that was waiting for us on Nebraska Street, in San Juan, TX.

We had all our possessions and our nine children in tow. The house had some furniture in it such as a stove, refrigerator, table and chairs. A living room suit, several beds, and we had a mattress in the car where the children slept on as we traveled. We were going to be just fine. We were doing the work of the Lord. We all settled in to start our new life. The children were registered for school and started immediately.

This was our family when we moved to San Juan, Texas
January 7, 1963
Back row: Melvin, John, Anna, Melvin Jr, Mervin
Middle row: Linda, Clair, Leroy
Front Row: Sarah, Anna Ruth, Carl

It was a whole new lifestyle, we had to learn to fit in. Melvin Junior's first day of school was a big learning experience. His new High School coach asked him a question and he answered "Yeah", the coach seemed to take offence to his response. Junior was confused, he didn't know what else to say. After being asked the question again and answering "Yeah" three to four times, the teacher became very agitated and got a paddle and came toward him, smacking the paddle in his hand saying, "Yeah what?" Junior said he was sorry, he knew the coach wanted a yes answer, but did not know what he was saying wrong. Finally, the coach yelled, you answer with "Yes sir" or "No sir, with his nose almost touching Junior's nose. He warned Junior that if he said "Yeah" one more time that he would be spanked. Being Pennsylvania Dutch, we were never taught to say, "Yes sir", if we did people would think that we were trying to be a smart aleck. We realized we would have some adjustments to make to fit into this new State of Texas.

REVIVAL MEETINGS IN MEXICO

The first Sunday in San Juan we were asked to help a Missionary in Progresso, Mexico in the afternoon service. We helped with a feeding program at noon. The service started and while the missionary was preaching, a horse and wagon drove up with a very sick lady on it. They came and got us and asked us if we could pray for her. The interpreter and I prayed for her and God healed her immediately. She stayed for the rest of the service. She could not thank us enough. We told her that it was the power of God, and we are only vessels of God. We are his hands extended. His mercy endures forever.

My interpreter and I praying for the lady on the wagon

The Missionary praying for the congregation

The following week we preached a revival in Reynosa, Tamaulipas, MX. The missionary's sixteen-year-old son was my interpreter and he was very good. We worked together very well. We had marvelous meetings, many people got saved and healed.

The next week we started a revival in, Rio Bravo, MX not very far away from our new home. More miracles and more people came to Christ.

From there we held a revival in a very small town called Tenosites, near Charco Azul, MX. The revival was a real success with many souls coming to Christ. The third day in the service, Anna got a revelation of two people in the church that if they didn't get their hearts right with God tonight, before the week was up, they will be in their graves. Two young men got up from their seats and said, "We know we are those two people, please pray for us, we are not ready to die." They were completely drunk. Both men gave their hearts to the Lord immediately, he even sobered them up. Later one of these young men became our first Youth Leader in Charco Azul.

Our services were across the street from a very religious church. A lot of their congregation came to our services and gave their hearts to the Lord, and that upset Satan. There was a gathering of angry people across the street that paid for those two men's drinks. They had encouraged them to get rid of the preachers. Their plans were to do so during the service. God had other plans for their lives.

The second week of the revival there were so many people coming, that the church building was much too small. They decided to build a brush harbor beside the church for the overflow. People from nearby villages asked me to bring them to the revival in my Station Wagon. I picked up as many people as I could. One evening when we got to the church, I counted thirty-two people pouring out of my Station Wagon. I don't know how they all got in.

The second night of the revival, for unknown reasons, the interpreter instructed me to move the bench forward that I was sitting on. Not questioning his reasoning, I obeyed. After a while I saw a man getting up suddenly from the congregation and rushing outside, we did not know what was going on. It turns out that someone had thrown a knife through the brush behind me to kill me. It missed me and stuck in the ground directly behind me where I would have been sitting if I had not moved. The man in the congregation that got up and rushed out, had seen the knife and ran around the outside of the brush harbor and removed it from the ground quickly, so I wouldn't see it. They thought that if I would see it I would not come back to preach the next night. Several men stayed outside during the rest of the services for our safety.

The meetings ended with great results. Many were saved and filled with the Holy Spirit, and many were healed by the power of God. It seemed like after the day of Pentecost. It says that there were added to the church daily such as were saved. The church about doubled in size.

WATER BAPTISM

Saturday night we announced there was going to be a baptismal service Sunday morning. Traditionally in Mexico, they have baptismal services on Easter Sunday. We did not have baptism pools in the church. We went down to the river or the canal like Jesus did. One lady that got saved in the revival, came to me and said, "I don't know if I can be baptized, or not? My life has been messed up for a long time. When I was a teenager, I married a young man that came through our village with the circus. We lived together for nearly two weeks. When the circus left town, he left with them. I have never seen him since. I have no idea whether he is dead or alive. I cannot get a divorce from him, as I know nothing about where he might be. She said, soon after that I began to live with this man that I am with today and together we have two children. I gave my heart to Jesus in the revival this week, and don't know what to do?" As you know, I was a member of a conservative Mennonite Church before I had received the Baptism of the Holy Spirit, so I did not know what to say to her. I told her that according to the way I understand the scriptures, I do not believe that she could be baptized. I told her that I would go home and pray and ask God about it, and I will bring the answer to her the next day at the Easter Sunday Service.

I went home that night and began to pray. I told God about her situation. I reminded God about how I understood His word. I could not sleep, I prayed even more earnestly. Finally, the Lord said to me, "If I accepted her, why can't you?" I said, "but Lord the scriptures say", the Lord cut me off and said again. "If I accepted her, why can't you?" I thought I was praying with an open mind, but sometimes our doctrines that we have been taught are more powerful than the Word of God, unbelievable but true. I said, "Dear God, please tell me what you mean". The Lord spoke again saying, "If I accepted her, why can't you?" I said, "please God show me what you mean." He asked, "Did she not accept me as her Lord and Savior into her life." I said, "I guess she did." He said, "Did I not fill her with the Holy Spirit, did you not hear her speaking in tongues?" I said, "Well, yes." Then he finished saying, "Then why can't you accept her?" I said, "Lord, show me your way."

Immediately I was reminded of the book of Acts, Chapter 10, verses 1 through 43 where an angel of the Lord gave Cornelius, a Gentile, a vision. Instructing him to send servants to Joppa, into a Jews home requesting him to come and teach them about his walk with the Lord. Cornelius knew that in those days, it was unlawful for a Jew to associate with a Gentile, but Cornelius obeyed God.

God prepared Peter, the Jew, in a dream that the two servants were coming and that he was to do as they asked. The Holy Spirit revealed to Peter that we are not to call anyone common or unclean, we are all brothers and sister in the Lord. Peter obeyed and as he spoke to the Gentiles, the Holy Ghost fell on them which heard the word and he baptized them in the name of the Lord.

The following day we got up early to go to Mexico. I found the lady I counseled with the day before and told her what the Lord revealed to me. I told her, "If Jesus can accept her, so can I." I told her that if she has Jesus in her heart and she desires to be baptized, I would be glad to baptize her. We baptized thirty-two people that day.

Afterwards we had a real feast. Everyone brought food to share at the canal. I never saw anyone slice a water melon like Bro Luna did that day. He cut it with a knife, just halfway through, from one end to the other. He continued to cut about 1-inch strips all the way around. He bumped it a bit, it fell apart and each slice separated perfectly. We had a wonderful time of fellowship that day.

I remember roasting hotdogs on a stick over an open fire. Some would get impatient waiting on the others to finish with the stick, so they threw the hot dogs into the fire cooking directly on the hot ashes.

Traditionally, the children would bring decorated flour eggs to smash on each other's head. The egg white and yolk would be removed from a small hole in the shell, dried, filled with white flour, taped shut and decorated. It was great watching them have fun. The children never got mad at each other with white flour throughout their hair and all over their face and clothes.

After the baptismal service, we were returning to the church on a single lane dirt road. It had just rained the day before, so the road was very muddy. Water holes were so deep sometimes the front of our car or pickup dropped into the hole in the road and mud and water came up over the hood.

Every so often there was a turnout, to let other cars pass. We were nearing the next turnout when a car came from the other direction. He didn't stop at the turnout, he pulled his car right in front of us, stopped, turned off the motor, lit a cigarette, and looked the other way. It was obvious he was not going to budge, he thought he would make us back up about a quarter mile to let him pass by. We came to an abrupt stop, Anna happened to be driving the front car, and I followed third in line, not sure what was going on ahead. I heard Anna call for the man driving the car behind her, he was six foot seven inches tall. She asked if he could come up to her car. He had to peel himself out of the car because of his size. He had very broad shoulders, when he stands up, everyone is going to feel intimidated. She asked him to come and let the guy see him. As he walked up to Anna's car, he started to roll up his shirt sleeves. The man blocking the road took one look at him, started up his motor and backed into the turnout very quickly. He never looked up as we were passing by.

CHAPTER 9
SPREADING THE GOSPEL

STARTING OUR FIRST CHURCH IN MEXICO

We started having services in a home of an elderly grandmother in Charco. Houses in Mexico were mostly dirt floors and no electricity. Open windows and doors were the only air-conditioning they knew. I remember one day in the middle of the service a mama duck came waddling through one door of the house and out the other with all her little duckling behind her.

After the service, her daughter invited us to her home for a meal. They peeled the potatoes, letting the peelings fall to the floor. Soon little piglets came in and cleaned them up. No need to carry out the garbage or sweep the dirty floor.

The family where we ate our first meal in Mexico

The people soon got permission to have services in the old tattered church building that sat vacant in the village of Charco Azul for several years. We soon filled the old church with new converts. The building was so old that you could see day light between the wall boards, which allowed for some air flow, at least the roof didn't leak. The congregation did not care that it was an old warn out building. Nothing kept the people from serving the Lord. It was so easy to preach to them, they were so hungry for the gospel. There was such a mighty outpouring of the Spirit of God, that nothing else seemed to matter.

The Church was just a one room building. Dirt floors, and rows of hard boards to sit on. There was no room for Sunday School classes inside, so the children were taken outside in the open air. The climate was so hot, there was no grass, only hard parched ground for the children to sit on. They did not care, they were so hungry for the Lord.

The government set aside approximately one thousand acres of land in Charco Azul. The project was called, Ejido Buena Vista, this was the Mexican welfare system. We would call it a co-op in the US. The Government would lease 15 Hectors (approx. thirty-four acres) of land to each family that could not afford to buy their own farm.

On the farms, most of the families grew cotton. The climate in Mexico is very hot and very little rainfall annually so irrigation is necessary for harvest. There are man-made canals everywhere to bring water to the farms, but the farmers must pay for the water they use, and most cannot afford it. When we arrived for services, their cotton crops were only a foot high and in full bloom, their yield would be very minimal without irrigation and would not cover the costs, less yet feed the family. They asked us to pray for rain. I had never prayed for rain before, but we prayed, and it happened. It began to rain the next day drenching the parched ground. Miraculously an abundance of rain fell on all the land of the co-op. The farms outside the co-op, barely got any. The cotton grew waist high, produced cotton by the bales.

The farmers now were so busy, they had no time to go to church, too much cotton to pick. Suddenly, the Boll Weevils (a worm that eats into the cotton bud and the bud will not open or produce cotton) got into their cotton crops. The harvest ended abruptly and the farmers all came back to church and repented. They realized that God had blessed them so much, but they neglected him. We prayed again for God to forgive them and have mercy. They had no money for pesticides, but the next morning the farmers went out into their fields, miraculously, the Boll Weevils lay dead all over the ground. The cotton continued to bud and yielded more cotton. They harvested an abundant crop that year.

There was no doubt in their mind that God gave them a miracle. The farmers had lost their credit in the bank because of crop failure previous years, so they could not borrow any more money for irrigation or pesticides. God blessed them with rain and killed the worms, so no money was needed for irrigation or pesticides, God provided. The farmers were able to pay off all their former debts, and they were able to buy farm equipment, as they were farming with horses before. God blessed them so much they soon started to tear down their mud huts and built lumber and cement block homes. The blessing of God came to Charco Azul. (Puddle Blue).

MORE OUTREACHES

I was praying to the Lord for more out reaches. The Lord began to open doors to share the gospel of Jesus Christ. We ministered in a village called La Posta, and during the service one night, the Lord showed me a vision of another village, a place I had never been or seen. The following evening, we headed out looking for it. We asked God to please direct our path. I was sure God would help me recognize it when I saw it.

As we were driving along, suddenly we saw a young man riding on a horse, as fast as it could go. He hollered to us, announcing that there was a man trapped in a well in the village ahead. He hurried on to get more help and we drove into the village to see if there was anything we could do. The villagers told us that a man was down in the well trying to make the opening at the bottom bigger, because the well had gone dry. While he was digging, it caved in on top of him. I asked if anyone went down to help him, they said no, everyone was afraid. I told them to tie a rope around me and I would go down. They looked at me as if I was crazy.

I asked my interpreter to preach to them while I was down in the well. I made it to the bottom and started digging. I filled the bucket many times. As fast as I removed the sand, the hole filled up again. I was getting nowhere but I did not give up. The sun went down and they got a flash light to shine down where I was working. They happened to bump the flash light, on the side of the well and it opened, dropping the batteries on my head, nearly knocking me out.

After several hours or so they called down to me and begged me to please come out. They felt there was no hope of finding him alive and there was no use putting my life in danger any longer. They told me an equipment company was coming with a large dragline and will get him out. I wanted to get that man out with all my heart, I did not want to give up, but realized it was no use. It touched their heart that an American would risk his life for one of theirs.

Later that night the equipment came, and they started digging from the top until they found the body, approximately thirty feet below ground level.

The villagers were so moved and asked me, if I could come back and preach. We arranged to return the following

Sunday. The meeting was in open air, under a tree, they did not have a church building. While I was preaching, suddenly I realized, this was the place the Lord had showed me in the vision.

One of the local men there in the village used to be a member of a large church in Reynosa. He had backslid from serving the Lord. He was one of the first to make a full surrender and committed his life to the Lord. He soon became the pastor of the group. It was not long, they were able to build a church building to worship in. Today that man's son is the pastor of the congregation.

THE DAY GOD MIRACOUSLY GAVE ME
THE SPANISH LANGUAGE

Several months later a pastor from Berlin Ohio announced that he would like to minister with us in Mexico. We took him to the village of Nuevo Evanito. That day my interpreter decided to drive his own car and meet us there. I arrived at the village with the Ohio pastor, but my interpreter did not show up. When it came time for church to start, the village pastor opened the service. The Ohio pastor and I did not understand anything that was being said, we just worshiped with them. The preliminaries were prolonged; more singing, more testimonies, waiting for the interpreter to arrive. I was praying to God to please send the interpreter. The pastor had already given me the hand gesture twice of what do we do now? I returned the hand gesture to him, I don't know. It appeared as if the pastor was about to dismiss the meeting. My heart was heavy, I was afraid the Ohio pastor would return home, and tell his congregation, that Melvin is not doing anything, he can't even speak their language. He had already told us that their church was thinking about sending financial support for the work in

Mexico. Maybe even send a family to help us in the work. I could not let him down, I could not let God down. I got on my knees and asked God to bring the interpreter now. I was praying desperately with all my heart. As I prayed, I reminded the Lord about several weeks prior, we were having a great service in open air and a rain storm was coming across the field like a wall towards us as we were worshiping the Lord. We stood and rebuked the storm and the storm instantly divided into two parts and went around us on both sides. I told God that he can perform a miracle again. I prayed, "If the interpreter's car broke down, Lord you can fix it. If he had a flat tire, Lord put air in the tire. Lord please send my interpreter now." The Lord interrupted my prayer and said to me, "you interpret". I said, "God how can I interpret, I cannot testify, I cannot preach, without an interpreter, and I have no understanding of what they are saying. How in the world could I interpret when I don't know the Spanish language?" The Lord spoke again and told me that I was to interpret. I got up from my knees and sat down beside the Ohio pastor. I asked the Lord to have the village pastor give me the sign one more time, and he did. I raised my hand with the gesture to wait a moment. I still could not understand what anyone was saying, but I stood up in faith.

That very moment, God gave me the gift of the Spanish Language.

The pastor from Berlin Ohio and I walked to the front where the local pastor was standing. He didn't move, he was confused, he just looked at us as to say, what are you going to do? The Ohio pastor began to preach, and I started to interpret. The local pastor was shocked. He stood there for a moment with his eyes wide open and his mouth dropped to the floor. Suddenly he realized he was still standing behind the table and jumped out of the way. The Ohio pastor preached a full message and I interpreted.

In this same village, during another Sunday afternoon service, the children were having Sunday School in the house next door when the Spirit of the Lord came upon them and they all received the Baptism of the Holy Spirit and were slain under the power of the Holy Ghost. It was very cold outside, so they had hot burning charcoals in the middle of the dirt floor to warm the house. Somehow, the hot coals disappeared. The children were laying all over the floor, none of the children were burned.

The Lord moved in the service outside as well, the adults received the baptism of the Holy Spirit. One young girl received the baptism and spoke in tongues in fluent English. She never spoke English before. As far as I know, she doesn't speak English today. God gave all of us a sign that day, just like in the book of Acts.

Acts 2:6 Now when this was noised abroad, the multitude came together, and were confounded, because that every man heard them speak in his own language.

I have been preaching and interpreting in Spanish ever since. English to Spanish or Spanish to English. I give my God all the credit, all the honor and all the glory for all the miracles he does and has done.

Romans 12:3 For I say, through the grace given unto me, to every man that is among you, not to think of himself more highly than he ought to think; but to think soberly, according as God hath dealt to every man the measure of faith.

Romans 10:17 So then faith cometh by hearing, and hearing by the word of God.

Ephesians 3:20 Now unto him that is able to do exceeding abundantly above all that we ask or think, according to the power that worketh in us.

God did not only give me the gift of the Spanish language, he also helped me to lose my former Pennsylvania Dutch accent. Spanish people thought I was a Mexican and could not believe that I was an American. My what God can do if we only trust him.

You can imagine all the mistakes one can make learning a new language. An American preacher was preaching his first sermon in Spanish and asked us to open our Bibles. He tried to say chapter 9 and verse 9 in Spanish, but he said "nieve", instead of "nueve". He changed the "u" to an "i", giving the word a whole new meaning, chapter ice cream, and verse ice cream.

One time I said, Jesus died on the cross of a horse (caballo), instead of the Cross of Calvary (Calvario).

I was also reminded when I learned to quote my first scripture verse by memory **Matthew 18:20 For where two or three are gathered together in my name, there am I in the midst of them.** Instead of saying "there am I in the midst of them (media)". I said, "there I am in the women's nylons (medio), only changed one letter. I am sure I made many more mistakes.

Learning a new language is a lifetime experience. I am still learning English, and I imagine I will still be learning Spanish as long as I live.

A MIRACLE AT HOME

One time our family finances had dwindled to nearly nothing. Several people had started to support us financially by this time, so we went to the Post Office every day hoping for some money to be there, nothing came. By the third day of looking and anticipating, we were a bit frustrated, our money was all gone. We went to the post office twice that next day expecting a letter still nothing. I told Anna that maybe we can go to the grocery store and purchase several things on credit. I am sure we will receive something by mail soon to cover it. We headed for the grocery store, we had never asked them for anything on credit before. We prayed and asked the Lord to help us in some way or another. On the way to the store, Anna said, "I feel like we are going to eat turkey for supper tonight." I said, "Anna we would never buy a turkey on credit." She repeated, that she still feels that we are going to eat turkey for supper that night. We arrived at the grocery store to find the store was already closed for the evening. I looked at Anna and said, "now what?" She said again, "I feel like we are going to eat turkey for supper tonight." By now I was quite discouraged, but Anna still had her faith high. It always seemed that if one of us seemed to have almost lost our faith, that the other one's faith was increased.

We turned around and headed for home. The cupboards were bare, not even milk for the baby. I figured that Anna and I can fast, some of the older children can fast, but what about the young ones and the five-month-old baby. How do you tell a baby, maybe tomorrow we will have some milk for you? As I was trying to reason in my thinking on what to do, we arrived home. All the children came running out of the house. They said, "guess what?" Anna interrupted and said, "there is turkey in the house." The children were astonished, how did she know they had turkey?

Our missionary neighbors had invited a missionary family of seven for supper that evening. Right before supper this family calls them and said, "please forgive us, my wife's mother just passed away in Louisiana, and we must leave immediately for the funeral services." Our neighbors had prepared a feast and decided to divide everything in half, including the turkey, all the trimmings the butter and milk, and delivered it to our home while Anna and I were on our way to the store.

The next day God provided us with a letter with a check of support that we were expecting. The Lord also provided a partnership business that provided funds to make it possible for us to go to Mexico more often, as well as pay all our bills on time. God is so good.

On another occasion, we were eating supper, (Dinner to city folks) but had no milk for the baby. Anna decided to go out to the building where we stored the clothing we had received for Mexico. Sometimes, there was change in the pockets of the donated clothing. She went through some boxes and in the last box she reached into a pocket and found seventy-five cents just enough for milk.

Anna was sorting clothing we had recently received. She opened one box, and was pulling out some clothes, when suddenly out rolled one hundred-thirty dollars. We checked with the people that had sent the boxes of clothes. They said that no one ever reported it missing. It was a miracle, it was enough to pay the rent and light bill coming due. God is so good, he is more than enough. ***Philipians 4:19 But my God shall supply all your need according to his riches in glory by Christ Jesus.***

TOO MUCH FOOD

I was invited to go to the state of Nuevo Leon into the interior of Mexico for a week of revival. I had three young American boys with me and one Mexican that knew where we were supposed to go. We ministered for several days and the Lord moved. The Lord spoke to me to go further back into the mountains.

On our way there we were hungry, we stopped along the road to eat some Campbell's Vegetable soup that we warmed with canned heat. We enjoyed it very much after a week of eating nothing but Mexican food.

We continued to the foot of the mountain, not sure where we were going, but following God's direction. We arrived at a house that the Lord directed us to. We introduced ourselves. The family was just ready to sit down to eat their noon meal and they insisted that the five of us sit down and join them. They did not know we had already eaten, but we felt compelled to eat, even though we were not hungry. They filled our bowls with a few noodles in chicken broth. The problem was that there was no silverware. Tortillas was the only thing we had to eat with. We soon found out that you must eat the tortilla with each bite and get a new piece for the next bite because it would get soggy and fall apart, it was very filling. When we emptied our bowls, they filled them again. We ate all the food they had prepared for their family, even though it was quite a difficult time of year for them, due to a drought in the area. They wanted to bless us.

After finishing the second bowl, they told us we needed to go and pray for a man next door dying of pneumonia. We arrived at his home. The weather was cold, and we noticed he was laying on a wooden pallet for a bed covered up with many blankets. We prayed for him, God miraculously healed him. He sat up and said, "now let's go to the kitchen." We knew what this meant, more food. We told him that we already ate twice, but he insisted we eat something. Again, they served us two more bowls of soup and tortillas.

When we were done, they asked us to go to their next-door neighbor and pray for a blind lady. The young men with me said, okay, but absolutely, no more food. We prayed for the blind lady. God answered our prayers. She was healed and was able to see. I asked her what color my shirt was, and she correctly said, blue. I asked what color my pants were, and she correctly said black. We rejoiced in the Lord!! Her daughter invited us to the kitchen. I apologized and kindly declined stating that we already ate three times and we cannot possibly eat any more food. Immediately, I realized she was offended. I went to her and said, "mam we will eat your food." I told the young men that we are going to the kitchen and don't ask any more questions. While we were eating her food, she came to me and said, "We Mexicans feel that you Americans are so much better off than we are. If our food isn't good enough for you, then your gospel isn't good enough for us. Now that you are eating my food, can you tell me how I can become a Christian like you." She accepted Jesus as her Lord and Savior before we finished two more bowls of food. We had no clue how we finished all the food. After this was all over none of us got sick or even suffered from gorging ourselves, God intervened.

We started a church there in the village. One of our first Bible School Students came from that village. She also became one of our first teachers. There are several ministers preaching the gospel of Jesus Christ from that village to this day.

A DEMON PASSESSED MAN DELIVERED

We started having church services in a home in a village called, Canales. The people in this village were very poor. The houses were nearly all mud huts, with dirt floors and palm leaf roofs. Several weeks after we started the evening service a man walked in very well dressed. We had no idea who the man was. We thought possibly he might be an Immigration Officer, so I asked one of the Bible School Students to preach, so there would be no problem. The officials always believe that the American Missionaries are taking the work and money from the Mexican people, which would be against the law. The well-dressed man sat there very respectfully through the entire service.

After the meeting was over he walked up to me and asked if I would please go with him to pray for his brother? I told him we would be glad to do so. He told us his brother is in a hut tied with a chain for thirteen years, completely out of his mind. He was working in a bank when he became very ill. He tried stabbing himself multiple times. I told the man that I believe that God would understand and that He would intervene.

As we got closer to the hut, we could hear the chain rattle inside the house. I was a bit nervous but not scared. We followed the man in and saw the man completely naked, looking more like an animal than a human being. We started pleading the Blood of Jesus. Rebuking every evil spirit that was possessing him. As we came near to him, he turned to get away from us as far as the chain left him. We continued to get closer, when suddenly he turned around and came flying towards me with his fingers like claws and his teeth like a lion. As he came for my neck, my hand shot out. The moment my fingertips touched his head, the man collapsed and fell to the dirt floor. The two students jumped over to help me pray as he lay there. We rebuked the demons and demanded them to come out of this man in the name of Jesus. His whole body relaxed, and God said the work is finished. Afterwards, his wife shared how they cannot keep him clothed. She showed us a pair of brand new blue jeans and explained how they would bind him and put them on him. Immediately he would rip them off from top to bottom with his bare hands.

They invited us to the house nearby where the wife was living. They served us some food and thanked us from the bottom of their hearts. The following week this man and his wife came to the meeting. He was completely healed and in his right mind. When the altar call was given, both Pancho and his wife came forward and accepted Jesus as Lord and Savior.

Several weeks later we left for the northern part of US for the summer to raise more financial support for the work in Mexico. While we were traveling, we received a message that the delivered demon possessed man had passed away. He and his wife were walking down the sidewalk in the city of Rio Bravo looking for a job. He looked at his wife and said, "Honey, I thank God that he allowed me to live long enough to be delivered from the power of Satan." Saying thank you to Jesus, for saving his soul, and he dropped over dead, right there on the sidewalk in the middle of town. I asked God why. I told God that this man could have been such a testimony to so many people. The Lord reminded me that this man was out of society for all these years. Besides all this, you can imagine how everyone that would see him that knew him as that demon possessed man might ridicule him and say, "that is that crazy (loco) man". God said, "I knew that he could not have stood the pressure of the present time, so I brought him home". I thanked God for another soul in the kingdom and trusted that God knew better than me.

This picture was taken the night
The delivered demon possessed man
and his wife gave their hearts to Jesus.
One week after his deliverance.

BEING IN THE RIGHT PLACE AT THE RIGHT TIME

Can you imagine, traveling annually to raise funds for the Mission work to the Central and East Coast of the United States during the summer months, with usually nine children. Driving from church to church for Sunday morning, Sunday nights, and sometimes every night of the week services. The children would sing songs in Spanish and I would give an update on the Missionary work and preach the Word of God. Anna was so good taking care of the children, keeping them occupied while I was preparing for the sermon. She made sure I got my rest, and kept us fed. The children were so patient and well behaved. One pastor told us the behavior of our nine children was unbelievable. All nine of our children cooperated much better than one daughter of the evangelist that was there several weeks prior. We were crowded, but we always made out great.

We were heading north to the State of Iowa for a convention. We normally traveled around the clock. Anna would take a shift driving, so we could continue and cut the driving time in half. That way it would not be a long and boring trip for the children. As we drove, the children would sleep, sing and play road games, like the alphabet game, finding the letters of the alphabet on billboards to see who can get from A to Z first, Etc... Around noon one day we looked for a rest area with picnic tables and room for the kids to play and run off some energy. When we stopped, I decided to play baseball with the children while Anna cooked a full meal for the family. She always knew how to make a fast meal great for everyone. She always made the trip enjoyable.

While we were playing baseball, I noticed two young men at another picnic table eating their lunch. They both had beer cans setting next to their food, trying not to be noticed. I kept an eye on them both. The one kept watching us. It seemed a bit strange for him to watch us so intently. We were having a great time with our game. I was the pitcher and referee. One of the boys hit the ball and it hit one of the girls in the face. She accusingly told him that he hit her on the cheek, when her brother, the batter said, "you are supposed to turn to the other cheek", like it says in, **Luke 6:29 "To him who strikes you on the one cheek, offer the other also. And from him who takes away your cloak, do not withhold your tunic either".** The man that was watching us so intently heard what they said. He got up from eating his lunch, came to me and told me he has been watching our family. There is something so different about us and thought we must be Christians. At one time he used to serve the Lord, but he backslid. He got involved in things he had no business doing. Me and my family's life got his attention. He asked if God can forgive a man like him. He said he was so sorry for all the sins he committed and asked for me to pray for him. The baseball game ended with the prayer of restoration of one man returning to Jesus. How sweet it is when people watch your life and conviction comes into their heart. You plant the seed, God brings the increase.

Another trip coming back from up north, we were coming through Alabama. Anna was driving our motor home on Route 10 on a twenty-mile-long bridge with no gas stations, towns or houses within the twenty miles of swamp land. We had a tire blowout somewhere about half way across. We were able to pull off the side of the road onto a restricted exit for the oil rigs in the swamp.

A man in a pickup came by, seeing we were having troubles and stopped to help. I told him that I think we can change the tire and get back on the road. I was looking for the jack, but it was nowhere to be found. The man said he was sorry, but he had an appointment and was running late. He advised me to not stay there, he said the mosquitos and alligators will eat us alive. He looked at his watch and then he looked back at me and said, "I was supposed to be getting married right now, but my girlfriend decided to marry another man instead of me." I witnessed to the man and told him that if she had this in mind, she may have done this later and hurt him even more in the end.

He seemed to be pressed for time and said again, "You cannot stay here." He got his jack from his pickup and said again that he must hurry, he needs to go. He jacked up the motor home and changed our tire. It was so hot, and he was sweating profusely. I kept ministering to him all the while. Finally, he seemed to relax, the anxiety seemed to have left him. When all was finished he looked at me and said, "Sir! you have no idea what you just kept me from doing, I mean you really have no idea what you just kept me from doing." We offered him some cold water and he was on his way.

Sometimes we wonder why some things happen in the most undesirable time and place. The Bible says that the steps of the righteous are ordered by God. That means EVERY step and circumstances, we only need to figure out the why.

CHAPTER 10
RAISING THE DEAD

LITTLE GIRL RUN OVER BY A FARM WAGON

One Saturday night I preached a powerful sermon on the Healing Power of God. We witnessed many miracles that night, people were saved, healed and filled with the Holy Spirit.

The next morning the pastor preached a sermon on faith. Someone came and told him there was an accident at the neighbor's house. The steel wheeled wagon rolled over the head of a small child and it looked really bad. The pastor went running to the home, he picked up the little girl. The child was not breathing and had no pulse. The pastor said, Brother High preaches it, now we need this miracle. They began to pray, nothing happened. The pastor said they must really pray. Together they rebuked the Devil, they rebuked death, commanded Satan to take his hands off her little body in Jesus name. They commanded life to come back into the little girl's body. She opened her eyes and smiled. All bones were healed, and her head was perfectly shaped. What a miracle, this stirred up a greater faith in all of us.

VERY SICK BABY GIRL

Several weeks later the older sister of this little girl along with some other boys and girls from our Bible School went with us to the mountains of Nuevo Leon, to a place called El Gato (The Cat) for a weekend of conferences. The meetings started Wednesday evening. The pastor's sister had a very sick little eighteen-month old girl. During the service the mother brought her sick little girl for prayer. She had not slept for days, she just cried. We prayed for her, and immediately she went to sleep. After the service the mother took her home. Immediately the child woke up and cried nearly all night. We had three services a day and every service the mother was there with her screaming child. The same thing continued to happen every time. On Saturday morning after the service the mother took the sleeping child home. She laid the girl in a homemade cradle hanging from the ceiling. This time, the girl stayed quiet, so the mother decided to stay home and get some rest and clean the house. She rested, got the house in order, cleaned the floor, and felt it was strange for the little girl to be quiet so long. She checked on her and found her body, cold and stiff. She grabbed the body and ran to church.

I was preaching when, the mother came busting into the church. Running to the altar screaming hysterically, carrying the lifeless body of her little girl in her arms. There was a girl in the service from Charco Azul, that the Lord had raised her sister from the dead several weeks prior. She got up and asked the mother, what was the problem? The mother cried, "my baby is dead!" The girl told her, "don't worry, we will pray for her. God will raise her from the dead." At the same time, the Lord spoke to me and told me to hold the body up towards Heaven. I said, "God she is dead." I could clearly see death. The Lord said, "I said the body!" I got down from the platform, stood behind the mother, reached over her shoulder and took the lifeless body from her arms. I held the little body up towards Heaven as God instructed. My back was facing the congregation. Before I even started to pray, the girl behind me screamed. It was the girl that had spoken to the mother and made her the promise that we would pray and believe she will be raised from the dead.

I opened my eyes to see what happened that made her scream. The little girl was looking into my face. So now you see, it wasn't my faith, I still had not even prayed so it was not my prayers, it was only obedience. I can only give all the credit to my God for all the miracles He does, has done and will continue to do.

The baby in El Gato that was raised from the dead.
One month later as we arrived in El Gato the mother was coming back on horseback from a 2 ½ hr trip she took with her little girl to another village over the mountain. Completely healed and normal

PASTOR DIES SINGING

We were in Brownsville, PA, south of Pittsburg. I have never seen more or greater miracles in my life in any one church, in the United States than in this one.

A lady came for prayer which had one leg shorter than the other. She had at least four or five inch build up on the sole of her right leg. The foot on the short leg was deformed and two third the length of the other. She told me that she is believing for a miracle. I told her she better remove her shoes before we pray, she obeyed. We prayed to God for a miracle. When we opened our eyes, both legs and feet were identical. She looked at her feet, cried and said, "Now I have no shoes to wear Sunday morning for Sunday School." What a marvelous problem to have. She came to church Sunday morning with bed room slippers on.

A lady at this church the previous year, had asked for prayer. She had a real desire to play the piano and couldn't. We prayed for her, and God gave her the gift, and she has been playing the piano in Church ever since.

Miracles were happening, their faith was very high. There was a man in the service which I sensed was demon possessed. I kept my eye on him for several nights as I preached. I was waiting for the right time for his deliverance. One night, he came to the altar for prayer I went to him and asked how he feels. He replied, "terrible." I asked him if he wanted to be delivered? And he said, "yes!" I laid hands on him and began to pray, when suddenly he began to speak in tongues. Immediately, I knew that this was from Satan. If you have the gift of discernment, this will make chills go up and down your back, but you never need to be afraid of it. I knew that I could not help him at this moment, it was not the proper time. I had to pray for direction. I left him and went and prayed for others. After a while I came back to him and asked him how he feels now, He replied, "terrible." I asked him if he really wanted deliverance? He said, "yes!" I laid hands on him and prayed. He again started speaking in demonic tongues. I again left him to pray for the rest of the people, still waiting for the correct time. The third time on the way back to him, I grabbed the pastor's hand and said, I need your help now. I stood in front of him on the platform, I asked no more questions, I laid my hands on that man's head proclaiming the name of Jesus. He flipped over backwards, somehow, I flew off the platform, landing on him. He was foaming at the mouth, cursing and swearing, sliding across the front of the church floor like a snake on his back. As we were sliding across the floor, I was rebuking the devil, commanding him to come out of him. This went on for quite a while. We had traveled more than twenty feet across the floor, when he passed out. His wife feared he was dead. I told her that she will soon see a miracle. Several minutes later, you could see the Glory of God come on his face. He began to smile. He repented, and God filled him with the Holy Spirit right then and there. A miracle only God can do.

Sunday evening was the last night of the conference. Service started as usual. A pastor from West Virginia lead us in a chorus:

> I'm up on the mountain, and I won't come down.
> Up on the mountain and I won' come down.
> Up on the mountain and I won't come down.
> Do Lord remember me.
>
> Chorus
> ///I'm climbing higher and higher and I won't come down///
> Do Lord remember me
>
> The Devil doesn't like it, but I won't come down.
> The Devil doesn't like it, but I won't come down.
> The Devil doesn't like it, but I won't come down.
> Do Lord remember me.

Suddenly he fell over with a heart attack. I rushed over to pray for him. The man that was totally delivered from demon possession the night before came beside me, everyone else just sat there in shock. I rebuked death. I knew that this was a direct attack from Satan to disrupt the meeting. The preacher was just making a bold statement singing his song, "The Devil doesn't like it, but I won't come down" and Satan definitely did not like it. Several minutes passed by when the pastor came to me and asked me if we should take his body to the parsonage? I told the pastor that he was in charge, this is his church and I will do whatever he wants. God taught me to always respect the pastor in charge. At the same time there was a registered nurse in the congregation, she got up and left the church and said to herself. "If they don't call an ambulance or a doctor, someone will be in big trouble, and it won't be me." She got into her car, started driving out of the parking lot. God spoke to her to go back into the service, she started to argue with God. God said the second time to go back into the service. She obeyed God as she realized it was him speaking so she returned. By this time, we had removed the body to the parsonage. The pastor and I called the wife and daughter and asked them if they want to call a doctor. They told us that he would not want a doctor. We asked them, "what do you want to do?" they replied, "let's believe God". We returned to the room where the body was laying. We rebuked death again and commanded life to come back into his body in the name of Jesus. Suddenly he opened his eyes. About fifteen minutes later he was back on the church platform praising God.

I gave three different altar calls that evening. The altar was full every time. The first one was for everyone who wanted to totally surrender their life to Jesus Christ. Another one was for all those who needed a miracle from God. The third one was for everyone who wanted God to use them and make a total commitment of their life to Jesus Christ. We never had time for the preaching that night, the Holy Spirit took over and did His thing.

THE DOCTOR COULD NOT SAVE HER

An American doctor came to help in the Mission Clinic in Guatemala. One evening a lady brought a 19-day old baby to the Clinic. The doctor tried his best to save the child's life. He said that the family waited too long to get medical help for this child. The doctor said that this child cannot live without a miracle from God. He gave the child enough adrenalin to revive a grown man, and she was not responding. Suddenly, the doctor announced that she was gone. My friend and I were praying on the campus when the missionary called us asking us to come to the clinic instantly? He asked us to pray for the child. We prayed to our Heavenly Father and said, "Please dear God, return the life back to this little child, in Jesus name." God did just that.

She was still in a very dangerous condition. The doctor injected I-V solution under the skin in six or seven places about the size of a chicken egg. He said that it was impossible to put it in the veins, because they were collapsed. He knew it would help, but it would take longer for her little body to respond to it. After a while the doctor said, "she is gone again, please pray for her." Again, the Lord answered our prayers. This happened five times. The last time she didn't respond like before. Finally, the doctor said, we must let her go, she has been gone much too long and she would have suffered severe brain damage if she would come back. Now we had a decision to make, will we give the body of the little baby back to the mother in this condition, or do we pray more and harder?

We decided to go against the decision of the doctor and continued to pray. After we prayed again, she responded. This time she was even much better. The doctor said that she may just make it. Miraculously, the next day the mother was able to take the baby home alive and in fair condition. The doctor was still very concerned about the child's welfare knowing the condition of the homes in the jungles, but we trusted God.

About seven years later, A lady came to the Mission

Clinic with a newborn for the Missionary to treat for some illness. The mother asked him if he recognized the older child, she asked if he remembered the baby the Lord raised from the dead five times here in the clinic, she said this is the little girl that God healed. The mother said, by the way, she did not suffer from any brain damage, she is one of the smartest in their family. She never had any problem whatsoever. You see, it is always better to obey the Lord in all things.

DOMINGO LOSOYA, JR DEATH EXPERIENCE

One day Domingo's wife noticed that he was walking differently. She asked him if he was ok and he told her that he was just a little tired. But as time went on she noticed that he was getting worse and took him to the hospital.

It was almost one in the morning when they arrived at the hospital. They checked his vitals, and everything seemed ok. They still took him into a room to run some more tests. He gave his cap to his wife and a kiss. Little did he know that kiss could have been his last kiss he ever gave her.

Domingo tells us that from that point on, that's all he could remember. His wife was still in the waiting room when the doctor called her, to tell her how her husband was doing. They told her that her husband was very sick, and only had ten minutes to live. The man's wife asked them what happened to him. The doctors told her that his organs were shutting down and his heart would be the last to go. The doctors told her that if she wants to see him for the last time she was able to go and say her last goodbye. They warned her that he would most likely be gone by the time she got to the room. But thank God, she went in, he was still alive. She saw him in a sitting position, looking upwards towards the ceiling with his eyes gray colored and his arms twisted together. As the wife walked up to her husband, she hugged him and said, "Lord into your hands I surrender him". She then turned and walked into the hall where the doctors were waiting for her. She asked them, why is he sitting up? The doctors got confused and rushed in. Over the speakers she heard the alarm for code blue and the doctors asked her to make her way to the Family Conference Room. Still in shock, his wife refused to go.

As she stood there in a daze a priest came up to her and walked both her and her son to the Conference Room, where they waited for the rest of the family to arrive. As their sons and daughters were arriving they only had questions and no answers as to what was going on with their father. The priest insisted that they say a prayer for him. The doctors came in and told the family that there was no hope that he can ever come back from this.

The family refused to accept it. Domingo's wife told the doctor that she wanted him to remain on life support and the doctors didn't want to listen to her. One of the daughters spoke up and told the doctor that three weeks prior, her father told her that if he was ever in a situation like this he would want to be on life support for at least two weeks. While they were having this conversation with the doctor they made their way to the ICU and were instructed to say their goodbyes. The doctor let them know, that their father had already died three times, and death was evidently very close again. The doctor told them that even if they would leave him on life support and he would happen to survive, he would be a vegetable, there has been too much damage to his brain, heart and organs.

The family fought for continued life support for him, all the doctors would say was no! Our Pastor Richard from the Lighthouse (My son-in-law) came to pray for him. As he put his hands on his chest and started to pray, "Lord may his body respond to your word". Domingo's wife saw his chest rise, taking a deep breath on his own. She told the doctor what she had seen. The wife explained that God would bring him back if we believed in him. To which the doctor said, "fine let's leave it up to your God". They continued life support and gave him a dialysis treatment. The third day, the miracle happened, the man opened his eyes and according to the doctor he did not suffer any damages.

Domingo tells his side of the story, that while the family was fighting to save his life, he was experiencing some unknown and unusual things that would be hard to explain in our mortal world. He said, "I first felt I was in a dream of green grass with beautiful green rolling hills. While looking around I saw a white picket fence on top of a certain hill. Curious as to what would be on top of this hill I started to climb it. As I finally reached the top I looked up only to see my biological father and two older brothers that had passed on before me standing on the other side of the fence. While standing there in shock, my father asked how I was doing and explained how it would be better for me to cross to the other side of the fence to be with them. Where I would no longer suffer but share in happiness with them. As I stood looking at them and the fence that was between us, I had to politely deny my father's request to join them. Explaining to my father that I was not suffering, and I had to stay on this side to find my family. As I was walking away I heard my brother begging me to come back and see how beautiful it was on the other side."

Domingo said, "I decided to turn away and go back down the hill. While walking down I felt someone take my hand and walk with me. As I turned to see who this person was, all I saw was this white robe with a cloth belt around it. Curious as to who this person might be I looked upward hoping to recognize the face. As to my surprise I could only see smoke covering this figure's face, it was not clear. Once we reached the bottom of the hill, the green grass had disappeared and the person who was walking with me left me in a pitch-dark place, to which I could not see where I was. Looking for anything or anyone, a big dark dog with bright red eyes and a face of a demon became clear. While staring straight into this dog's eyes I felt the desire to pray to my Lord to save me from this dark unnatural place. By the time I opened my eyes I was in an animated colorful place, to which I saw an animated truck, the driver asked me to get in, so he could give me a ride. After what seems to be a very long ride, I opened my eyes only to find that I was inside a hospital room."

"I could see a nurse noticed that my eyes were open, and she was in shock to find that I was up speaking and alert. As I looked at the nurse the only words I could say was, "where is my wife?" They asked me what my wife's name was, to which I responded correctly. They rushed to call her, and she came in the room with a sigh of relief on her face and says to me "Hi honey, let me kiss those beautiful lips of yours."

Domingo was in the hospital for 15 days and his wife never left his side. He was so grateful to God that he had mercy on his soul and gave him life and his family back."

A LADY RAISED FROM THE DEAD

I was asked to pray for the wife of a pastor that now preaches to the people from the Food Pantry on our Home Base. We were told that she was in the hospital on full life support. Another pastor and I went to pray for her. As we were about to go into the room, my Lung Specialist was coming out. I asked the doctor how she was doing. He said for eighteen days this woman has had absolutely no brain waves. She is gone. He did not understand why the family doesn't just pull the plug. I walked into the room and said, "she shall live and not die." Then we prayed for her in Jesus name. The next morning, she opened her eyes recognized her husband sitting next to the bed and asked how she got there. She came out of the hospital, living a normal life to this day. The doctors don't know it all. God has the last word.

MAN DIES AT THE ALTER

We were in revival in the home church, The Lighthouse, in Donna, TX on 9-11. A friend of ours was returning from a mission trip in Mexico. He was planning to fly straight home to Florida. As they were arriving at the Harlingen Airport, the airport was closed. They had no idea what had taken place in NY at the Twin Towers and in Pennsylvania. They decided they needed to stay the night and arrived at our home base. Revival was in progress, and they came in and sat down. The Evangelist started to pray for the people. He prayed for this man, and he fell to the floor. The Evangelist thought he fell under the power of the Holy Ghost and began to rejoice. I kept trying to get his attention. Finally, the Evangelist noticed me and asked me what I wanted. I told him the man is dead. He asked, "What?" I said again that the man is dead. The man's wife was a registered nurse. She looked at me and said, "he is dead." She got her medical instruments to make sure. After checking him out, she confirmed that he was gone. By this time, his color was gray. We began to pray and rebuke death. Soon he opened his eyes and was okay. His wife being a registered nurse decided we better have him checked out. She knew being a registered nurse she could be in trouble if something happened, so we called an ambulance. The only thing they could find at this point was his blood pressure was high, everything else was okay. God did it again.

CHAPTER 11
ARRESTED

THE BIBLE SCHOOL WAS BORN

We had many young people that felt the call of God in their lives, so we decided to start a Bible School. People from other churches heard that the Holy Spirit was doing such a marvelous work through our Ministry. Many of their young people wanted to be a part of it as well as other pastors. So, the Bible School was born.

Within several years we had seventy-two students in our Bible School, as well as seventy-six churches that were looking to us for direction and leadership. The Lord was blessing us. Our church and dormitories were too small. We had students sleeping on the church floor, as well as in an old bus sitting on the property. Imagine, the sleeping conditions in the cold and the heat (thirty degrees to the heat index of one hundred-fifteen degrees).

Three sisters from, Matías Romero, Oaxaca, came to our Bible School. They had begun to sing as a trio when their father held revivals in different churches, they sang beautifully. We started a radio program in Matamoros, Tamaulipas. I was preaching, and they were singing. One of the sisters wrote a song for the introduction of our program. I will translate it as to what it says, in Spanish.

The church of Flame of Truth,
shall triumph, shall triumph.
The church of Flame of Truth,
shall triumph, shall triumph.

By the grace of God, omnipotent,
We must put forth much effort to overcome.
By the grace of God, omnipotent,
we must put forth much effort to overcome.

Spanish
La iglesia Flama de la Verdad
triumfará, triumfará..
La iglesia Flama de la Verdad
triumfará, triumfará.

Por la gracia de Diós Omnipotente,
deberemos enforsarnos pará poder vencer
Por la gracia de Diós Omnipotente,
Deberemos enforsarnos pará poder vencer

We had marvelous results from the radio program. Many students heard about us from the program and registered to attend the Bible School. We received many invitations to minister in other churches through this broadcast.

That same year we had a pastor from Tejuantepec, Oaxaca contact us about a young girl that arrived in his village from San Baltesar, Oaxaca, several hours away by bus. He begged us to accept her into our Bible School. Our rule was, the student must be at least sixteen years of age as well as have no less than two years of school education. She had neither, she never went to school and was only fourteen years old. He begged me to make an exception for her. The pastor said she accepted Christ at his church, and her family is very religious and has rejected her with her new-found Christianity, and she was too young to be away from home alone. He promised that if she cannot make it in Bible School, that he would personally come and get her. We made the exception.

To everyone's surprise she did well and made it through all eight months of classes. When summer vacation came, she decided to go back to minister to her own village. Two months later, she called the pastor from Tejuantepec, and asked him if he could please come and baptize all the converts there. She told the pastor that her parents as well as her Grandparents, brothers and sisters, and nearly all her cousins have accepted Christ and want to be baptized. What a harvest of souls by a fourteen-year-old miracle girl.

We helped build the first church there in her village. The following year her brother, as well as several of her cousins attended the Bible School. Her brother is now pastoring the local church in their village. We have visited the church numerous times. They soon out grew the church building we built for them and had to build a much larger building.

Our son Melvin High, Jr, recently visited their church. He told us that on Sunday morning there were 500 people inside the church as well as about 500 outside. They started several Missions in the mountain regions as well. One of the Missions is even larger than the home church.

BEING ARRESTED

The work and Ministry became much larger than we could handle. Our native Director of the churches in Mexico told me time and time again, to get someone else to relieve him of his position. He said, "I am just an uneducated man from the ranch, I can't do it." He was a real honest man of God but felt very incapable. Our Board of Directors on the US side got together to pray, as the Mexican Leaders had asked us to. We sought direction from the Lord, without God we can do nothing.

During that time a young man was attending the Bible School and began to help me with the leadership responsibilities. We were having abundant results and made a great team. The Board of Directors and I decided to promote this young man to relieve our native Director of the Churches of, Flama De La Verdad. (Flame of Truth in Spanish). Everything went well until jealousy rose up in the local church leader's hearts. They did not approve of our new Director of Churches and were afraid of losing their position and power. They decided to get rid of me and keep everything for themselves.

The disgruntled leaders of the local churches recruited 4 very influential men from the village to go to Mexico City and fill out a report at the Immigration Office falsely stating that there is an American man holding young people hostage in what they call a Bible School.

Dissention became so strong, we had to move the Bible School to Rio Bravo for a short time until we purchased a piece of land near Soledad. We left the former leaders have all the churches that wanted to remain with them. Thirty-two churches refused to stay under their leadership and wanted to stay with us. The new leaders convinced me to re-register Flame of Truth in Mexico.

One day we were celebrating Thanksgiving with the orphans, students and some of our supporters from Houston, TX. An immigration officer showed up and arrested me and told me that my name was in the Black Book (List of Illegal Americans) two times. After detaining me for twenty-two hours, he released me and threatened me to never return to Mexico. As you know God had a plan far above that which we can imagine or even think.

I thought my work was finished in Mexico and started to make plans to return to Pennsylvania. While we were packing things up, two Mexican brothers came by. One was the Director of our Bible School, the other was the newly appointed Director of Churches. They asked me what I was doing, and told me that I cannot leave them, they needed me. I responded that the Mexicans hate me, and I am leaving. They continued to say that they don't hate me, they love me. There are only a few that are jealous and want what I have and would do anything to get it. They pleaded for me to stay.

Several weeks went by and a man came to our door and said, "I am a Christian lawyer from Mexico City. I know that you do not know me, but I heard that you are having some problems in Mexico. I came to help you." I asked him how much it will cost? He said, "I am sent to help you, it will cost you nothing. If you will give me permission to go to the Immigration Office in Mexico, I will investigate." I told him that the Immigration Officer that arrested me showed me the Black Book from Mexico headquarters that my name was in there two times, I saw it with my own eyes. He returned several hours later and said, "You won't believe this, I asked the head official if I may see the book? I told him I was a lawyer from Mexico City, and showed him my credentials. I was permitted as your lawyer to see the book. I searched the book with all the names in alphabetical order and your name was not there. I asked the officer that if a name is no longer in this book, where is it? The officer told him that it stays in the book for five years, then it is removed and placed in those filing cabinets against the wall permanently. I asked the officer if I could see the files and he approved.

There were approximately forty or more, four drawer filing cabinets against the wall, again in alphabetical order. I found the file with all the names that start with H and your name was not there either. You can legally return to Mexico any time you want." Seems like he must have been an angel sent from God. Who else could cause my name to disappear from the book and all the Immigration historical records.

CHAPTER 12
RETURNING TO MEXICO

I went back across the Mexican border, all was well. God had performed another miracle. The Bible School began to increase again. Churches that left us to stay with the other leaders, were asking us to come back and hold revivals. The first group of churches that split off, have had many problems in their fellowship and have had several splits since then. God began to bless us all over again. We had all the churches we could handle.

REVIVAL IN MINATITLAN

I remember very well the open-air revival meetings in Minatitlan Veracruz. It was a large parking area near the river front. We had two hundred or more people attending. We had many give their hearts to Jesus Christ. We had many miracles happen there. A small brother and sister about nine and ten years of age came to the meeting. They both were completely deaf and dumb, they were able only to make grunting noises when they needed something. After prayer, both were healed and instantly they were able to speak and hear perfectly. This started a real revival. People began to repent from their sins and many miracles followed.

The revival continued as we made our way up the river. We had marvelous meetings in Salinas. From there we went further up the river to Hidalgotitlan, the Municipality of the whole area. It is like the County Seat in the US. Many Bible

School Students came from there, so we started a church for them.

The revival fires spread all over the southern part of Veracruz. Many churches were started all over the southeastern part of Veracruz and into the neighboring states of Chiapas, as well as in the state of Oaxaca. The revival had a great impact.

A TRIP UP RIVER

The Pastor in Minatitlan Veracruz was not only pastoring the church, he was also our Coordinator for the State of Veracruz. He started a radio program in Minatitlan Veracruz. One day during the radio program he had some visitors. After the program was over, they introduced themselves as people from El Mirador, Tabasco. They said there are quite a few people from their village that got saved because of this radio program. They told him that they do not have a church, or pastor there and asked if he could come to El Mirador and teach them how to live a Christian life and serve God. The pastor notified us, and we planned a trip to visit with them. It was nearly two hours by road, then approximately two hours up the river. The people responded to the gospel very well. They were so hungry and eager to hear the word of God. We were able to establish a church there.

We prayed for God to show us who he has chosen to be their leader when we are not able to be here. After prayer, the people told us that one of their group members has been doing his best to direct them and to teach them, but they are so new in Christ and they do not understand the scriptures very well. They said they also need Bibles, but only several can read. We made a commitment to help lead them and get Bibles for them. The church grew mightily, nearly everyone in the village was getting saved. They had one problem, there was a bar owner in town nearly going out of business due to everyone accepting Christ, and he became very angry.

We were invited to take another trip back to the Minatitlan village to baptize more converts. The trip was planned, but the night before we were supposed to leave, one of my sons had an accident with our family car. At the last minute, I could not go so I asked a brother from Canada that was visiting at our house, to go in my place. He took our pickup and camper with a group of leaders. On their way they stopped and picked up the radio Pastor from Minatitlan Veracruz.

In the middle of the service a man came into the church with a shot gun and a machete. He tried to shoot two times, but the pastor kept pointing his finger at the gun commanding it not to fire, and it did not. So, he got even angrier and pulls out the machete, knocks the kerosene lamp onto the ground as he was swinging it around. He pulled the machete back to hit the Canadian Pastor on the head. There was a piece of rafter sticking out from the side of the ceiling that the machete first made contact with, and it turned the blade sideways. The side of the blade hit the pastor's head, partially cutting off his ear. Still hanging on by the skin, they prayed, and God gave them a miracle and restored the ear like nothing happened. By this time the kerosene lamp that was knocked to the floor was completely out, and they were left in the dark. Everyone scattered in fear for their life. After a while when everything settled down and got quiet, some of the people got another lamp and went back into the church to check out the destruction that had taken place. They heard a noise outside, so two men went out with a flash light to see what was going on. Suddenly, they heard a noise on the ground right in front of them. They turned the light to the ground, just several yards from where they were standing was a shot gun pointed at them. This time it fired and hit one man directly into the heart and killed him instantly. Everyone else stayed hidden for the night. The next morning, they had a funeral for the first Christian Martyr in El Mirador.

We were told later that the bar owner had offered a large bounty and free alcohol for the one who would kill the Leader of the Group. This probably would have been me had my son not had the accident with our family car.

The bar owner ordered the people that were not saved to burn down all the houses of the people that went to the church. Many nights the people slept in the trees with their children in fear.

God used the death of that Christian man and blessed the village. The government offered some land in another area for all the Christians to live in peace. The congregation moved their families and formed another village. I had the opportunity to preach in that village, what a blessing. There was only one problem, there was no one there to share the good news of Jesus Christ with. There was another village close by where the gospel was badly needed, so they had their own Mission Field next door.

You see that God has a plan much bigger than ours. Sometimes we do not understand why certain things happen. Sometimes we do not listen when God speaks. I didn't know why my son had the accident. I had no idea I was not supposed to go on that trip. I had no way of knowing what was about to happen. God knew, and he worked it out. We must trust that God is in control and knows what is best.

Romans 8:28 And we know that all things work together for good to them that love God, to them who are the called according to his purpose.

THIRTY-TWO RECEIVED THE HOLY SPIRIT

A conference in Matias Romero, Oaxaca started out great. The meetings were held outside because the building was way too small to hold all the people. They had come from many villages around the area. Some as far as several hours by bus, and some riding in small cattle trucks. The day services were mostly teaching the Christians how to live a victorious life. The evening services were Evangelistic type where I ministered. The Holy Spirit was moving greatly. Many miracles happened every night. People got saved in nearly every evening service. Thirty-two, Born-Again Christians received the Holy Spirit at the same time, speaking in the heavenly language.

BAPTISMAL SERVICE IN OAXACA

Sunday morning, we had a Baptismal Service. After I baptized the converts, I gave another altar call. A man came forward, walked down into the river where I was baptizing, I asked if he had Jesus in his heart and life? He said, "Yes, I do, I just did not know for sure whether I was able to walk the Christian life or not. I know I am ready now to give up everything of the world for Jesus." I baptized him.

I asked if there was anyone else. Another lady left everything at the water's edge and came in to be baptized. She said I also am born again and ready to give up everything in my life for Jesus. The Pastor called me John the Baptist. I was called many things in life, but never was I called John the Baptist.

GRANDMOTHER, MOTHER, DAUGHTER DELIVERED

Before the afternoon services on the last day of the conference, the pastor asked me to go with him to visit a family, the grandmother was very sick. As we prayed for her, the Lord healed her. That evening the grandmother brought her daughter and her granddaughter to the meeting. When the altar call was given, the grandmother brought her daughter and granddaughter to the altar. They placed the five or six-year-old girl on the platform in front of me. I asked them what was wrong with her. They said, she is totally deaf and cannot speak at all. She makes a very low grunting sound if she wants something. I laid my hands on her ears and throat and prayed, "Devil, I command you to take your hands off this little girl in the name of Jesus. I rebuke you Deaf and Dumb Spirit to come out of this child in the name of Jesus. Lord you can form or heal these vocal cords in the name of Jesus. You can create an ear drum or whatever is missing in this child. Lord cause this child to hear and speak in the name of Jesus amen." I turned the girl facing her mother and said. Dile mamá (say mama) She said mamá just like any little girl would. Her back was to me, to make sure she could not read my lips, she heard exactly what I said and knew exactly what she was saying as she said it, looking at her mother. Immediately the mother and grandmother fell on their knees and asked Jesus to come into their hearts.

TIGHT SQUEEZE ON A NARROW BRIDGE

We were traveling with three pickup trucks loaded with Bible School Students going across a narrow bridge at Tampico, MX, before they had super highways. We saw a horse pulling a trailer made with a car axle coming towards us. We saw a tractor trailer coming up behind the horse cart at a high rate of speed. The driver must not have seen them until it was too late. He slammed on his brakes. His trailer must have been empty because it jack-knifed and was coming sideways toward us. We slammed on our brakes. Miraculously, that tractor trailer straightened out. Squeezed right between us and the horse cart and hit or scratched no one. We sat there for a bit in shock. We looked at the bridge, and at the horse and trailer and wondered how it was possible for that tractor trailer to fit between us. We could not do the math, it was not humanly possible. There was absolutely no explanation, it was clearly a miracle. Only God could squeeze a large eight-foot-wide eighteen-wheeler into a four-and-a-half-foot space. If God can move mountains, then this was a small feat.

A DRUNKEN MAN SOBERED AND HEALED

We were ministering in San Baltazar Oaxaca for several nights with great results. After Friday night we left to go to Jaltipan, Veracruz driving nearly all night for a weekend conference starting the next morning. In the evening service I started to minister. A man got up and began to walk to the front, he was staggering drunk. Two men from the congregation got up, grabbed the man and started taking him out of the service. I stopped them and asked them to bring him to me. They told me that he was drunk, and I replied that God will sober him up. The drunken man told me that he was in a fight with several men and they cut him in the leg with a machete and he wanted prayer. I began to pray as the Lord directed me. I said, "Dear Jesus, sober this man up completely. Father I want this man to get saved and heal him in the name of Jesus." I said, "Father if this man ever desires a drink again, that at the smell of the bottle it will cause him to get so sick that he will never be able to drink again in the name of Jesus." I instructed him to go and sit down and listen to the Word of God. He turned to go to his seat no longer staggering drunk. I didn't hear from this man until eleven years later.

The pastor of Oteapan, Veracruz invited me to preach his first night of revival in Jaltipan, Veracruz. I ministered that night on the Baptism of the Holy Spirit. When I invited the people, who wanted to receive the baptism, the pastor of that church came forward. When I prayed for him, he fell on the floor speaking in tongues being filled with the Holy Ghost. One hour later we picked him up and nearly carried him home. He was so drunk in the Spirit, he couldn't walk. While we were carrying him home he said to me, "I know that you do not know me, but I know you." He asked me if I remembered the drunk that I prayed for many years ago in the church across town, he said he is that man. He asked if I remembered how I prayed for him, he said exactly two weeks after I prayed for him he had all he could take and decided to get drunk. He went to the bar, bought a drink, picked it up to put it to his mouth when suddenly, he began to throw up. He ran for the door, he was never so sick in all his life. He went back to the church where I prayed for him and gave his heart to the Lord Jesus Christ. God called him into the ministry, and he is now the pastor of this church. You may never know what God can do with your prayers. Exactly as I had spoken in my prayers, so it happened. It pays to listen and obey God.

CARJACKED BY THIEVES

One evening we were coming home from a church service in Valley Hermosa. About thirty miles south of the Mexican border. It was a very dreary, rainy night. Suddenly,

we saw in front of us in our drive lane a Federal Highway
Patrol Car without lights on. As we all hollered at our driver
to stop, he swerved around them to avoid collision. Instantly
they began to follow us with all the lights flashing. Our driver
pulled to the side of the road and stopped. An Officer got out
of the Patrol Car and came up to the door and asked to see
his license in Spanish. The driver did not understand any
Spanish, and God told me to not say a word. The Officer
insisted to see his license. Finally, the driver realized what
he wanted and pulled out his wallet and gave him his
license. The Officer looked at him and at his license and
gave a hand signal as to wait a minute. He went back to the
Patrol Car as if he was checking things out.

I thought to myself, that I never saw a Federal Police
Officer that young before, and wondered why a Patrol Car
would be parked in the middle of the highway with no lights
on? I began to feel like something was not right. When the
young Officer came back to our car, the Holy Spirit hit me,
without thinking I grabbed the door handle, I flew out of the
car and hollered to them in Spanish. I said, "there is a
problem here and I will find out what it is." When my feet hit
the ground facing the Patrol Car, I met eyes with a man
about six feet tall with a long black trench coat holding a big
machine gun in his hand. Suddenly, he slammed the
machine gun inside his black trench coat and ran to the
Patrol Car. At the same time the young man dressed in a
Federal Police uniform threw the driver's license in the
window and ran back to the Patrol Car. I have no idea what
they saw or heard. Whether it was because my Spanish was
so perfect, and they thought this may be a setup, that took
them by surprise, or the bold action I took and my
authoritative voice. Maybe a huge Angel or Jesus himself
appeared before their eyes. Whatever they saw they were
afraid and they spun the Patrol Car around and headed
back to town in a hurry.

As the dust settled, I had a hard time keeping my heart down my throat or to stop it from beating out of my chest. I had no fear before, God gave me the power and authority over Satan. When the reality hit that they were not Police Officers and were there to rob or kill us, we headed straight for the border as fast as we could. God is our deliverer.

A DANGEROUS TRIP TO THE JUNGLES

There was a village way up the river in Veracruz, MX where most of the people that lived there were fugitives. This was a place where even the police were afraid to go. There was only one way to get to the village, you had to go part way on boat, and the rest was a couple of hours by foot. It was almost like a crooked tunnel of rocks on both sides of a deep gorge. One time thirteen Police Officers decided to go there to arrest one man. That man disarmed thirteen Police Officers by himself. He sent them back without their weapons and threatened that if they ever tried to come back they would be killed. The police never tried to return.

There was a Christian man from Soledad selling house wares that traveled to that village many times. Everyone else was afraid to go there. He invited a pastor and his wife and a young lady to go and preach a revival in that village. This man had notified the fugitives in the village that he was bringing them for a revival and they agreed to accept them.

The salesmen guided them to the village. They were scheduled to arrive in the evening, but traveling was very difficult, and they arrived the following morning. Later the salesman announced that he was leaving, he made sure they knew how to find their way out of the village on their own.

The salesman left the village alone, and when he arrived back at the gorge he decided to go down to the river to get a drink. As he was drinking he heard a voice behind him say "Turn around slowly and carefully." The salesman turned around looking into a double barrel shotgun. The fugitive man said, "You are one of them Hallelujahs. I am going to kill you. You told us that you were bringing them last evening, but you lied. A group of us were waiting here for you. Our plans are to kill the men and take the women hostage to be our wives. No one will leave this village alive."

The salesman said, "You know me, I am the salesman who comes here monthly to sell house wares to all of you. I am their guide, I am not one of them." The fugitive man said, "If I ever find out that you are one of them I will kill you." After much persuasion he left him go.

The salesman went back to Soledad, told the church what the fugitive man told him. All the people in the church began to fast and pray, night and day. They feared they will never see them again.

The revival services started in the village. The second night the Lord spoke to the pastor to announce to the fugitives that the meetings will continue another night. The pastor, his wife, and the young woman still knew nothing about the plan of these ungodly men. At midnight the Lord woke all of them at the same time. God said, quietly flee for your life. The pastor said to the Lord, "You said another night of revival." God said, "Go now." They got their things together and left quietly, not even a dog barked. With one small flashlight they found their way out to safety.

When they got back to Soledad, everyone was excited to see them. The people told them what was plotted against them. The pastor said God woke them up at midnight and told them to leave now, and they did not know why. God spared their lives, they just had to obey.

CHAPTER 13
UNDER ARREST AGAIN

A HOME FOR ORPHANS

We purchased some land and started to build another Bible School near a town called Soledad. As soon as we had the buildings under roof we moved the students. We had additional room and decided to open an Orphanage which was needed in that area.

The first year we had around twelve children. The following year, the Orphanage increased to eighteen. We had a one-month old baby girl brought to the Orphanage. Being there for only two weeks she became very ill. One day our oldest son took supplies to the Orphanage and discovered how sick she was. He called me and said that the baby is very sick, and he is bringing her home with him to take her to the doctor in Pharr, TX. We met him at the border of Mexico to get permission from the Immigration Office. They granted us permission and we took her to the doctor. The doctor said that she would probably not make it, she is more dead than alive. Thank God through the doctor, prayer and faith she made it through. We took her back to the Orphanage.

Two weeks later she was worse than the first time. Our son brought her home again. The doctor said that there is no hope, she was dying. Her intestines were so inflamed from her mouth to her bottom. The only thing that we were permitted to give her was Sprite. I asked the doctor how she can survive on just Sprite. The doctor said that the possibility of her surviving was next to none, but the Sprite will heal the lining of her stomach and intestines. He warned us that we needed to stay awake all night to watch her, she is so weak and does not have enough strength to cry. The doctor was a Christian man and he told us we needed to pray for a miracle. God gave us that miracle, she made it through. The Sprite healed her intestines, and soon she was able to drink milk and gain her weight back. This time we kept her at our house until she was completely well.

We were filled to capacity in the new school. We had room to grow, but construction on the other buildings was not completed, so we could not use them.

Everything went great for about five years. Americans are not legally permitted to own a business in Mexico, so we had to entrust our native Director to handle the finances and we put the Flama De La Verdad Mexico Ministry in his name. We provided the support money and he handled the finances. We provided money for groceries to feed the Orphans as well as the Bible School Students, and to forward the support money to several pastors in Vera Cruz.

A young couple came from Houston, TX to help at the Orphanage. They stayed for several days to help care for the children. They were US born Mexicans, so they spoke Spanish as well as English. Their church in Houston was a tremendous blessing to our Ministry in supporting the Bible School and Orphanage with food supplies and money every month. This couple knew exactly how much the Director was receiving from Flame of Truth in Texas, so they were concerned when they saw that the Orphans and Students were eating rice, beans, and tortillas only for every meal. They started to ask questions and in great fear, somebody told them the truth. They reported to us that the Director had threatened all the students and the orphans, that if they would tell anyone what they were eating, that he would deal with them harshly as well as dispel them from the school or orphanage.

At the same time, two pastors from Veracruz contacted me asking why we stopped their monthly support we had promised them, without notification. We again suspected that the Director was not being an honest man, and we had to approach him. I had sent the pastors a letter and asked them to meet me at the Bible School. We scheduled a time for the Director to meet us at the Bible School as well. I called a meeting with our Board of Directors at our San Juan, Texas office. We met for six or seven hours to discuss how we were going to best handle the situation. The Mexican Director called every hour asking Anna when we were coming over. Little did we know what was before us. Finally, Anna called and told him that we will be leaving in about fifteen minutes. We crossed the border at Nuevo Progresso, everything seemed normal. We found out later that he arranged for someone at the border to watch for us and to notify the head Immigration Officer when we were crossing. We arrived at the Bible School, and as the eleven Board of Directors, and I were getting out of our cars. Another car pulls up behind us. Out stepped the head Immigration Officer demanding to speak to Melvin High. I responded and walked up to him. He asked me if I was armed. I told him that I was not, that I do not even own a gun. He told me that he was told that I was heavily armed and dangerous. About the same time a Federal Highway Patrol Car came out of the field next door that was monitoring the situation, in case the Immigration Officer needed backup.

TAKEN AWAY

The Immigration Officer arrested me and put me in his car. I was not able to say anything to the pastors, the students or the orphans. My oldest son Melvin Jr followed me in our car. The rest of the Board Members also followed in their cars as the officer had ordered. He took us to Matamoros, MX. On the way he told me that someone in the group is against me. I shared some details with him as to what was going on, and the reason all the Board Members were with me, but he did not seem like he cared to hear what I had to say. He took me into an office and told me to sit down. He said, "you know Mr. High that it is illegal for you to be working in Mexico. You are violating the laws of our country. I could take you to prison now." I was interrogated inhumanely for three hours and forty-five minutes. He knew how to torture me with words I did not even know existed.

He released me and told me to cross the border to the US and never return to Mexico. I was so shaken, I prayed for God to please help me forget the torture. I can tell you that God is faithful, the only thing that I remember is one threat. He told me if he ever caught me in Mexico, he will personally take me to the Political Prison in Mexico City where I would never get out, not even my dead body, they will bury me inside the walls. I do not know why that memory still lingers, maybe only as a testimony. But I thank God that all the memories of the rest of the interrogation are gone. God alone can do a miracle like this. I give him all the glory, the praise and the honor.

IMMIGRATION FOUND US IN PA

The little one-month old girl that was dying from the orphanage, was still with us. We could not take her back to Mexico now, we had fallen in love with her and could not give her up, so we decided to adopt her. While we were going through the adoption process, we took her with us on our annual trip to Pennsylvania, raising funds for the Mission Field.

The Mexican Director reported us to the Mexican Immigration stating that we kidnapped a little girl from the orphanage and he did not know where we took her. He gave the Immigration Officials the address where we were staying in Pennsylvania. They tracked us down, finding Anna at a laundromat in Lancaster. He threatened to take the little girl back with him. We told him, that according to the documents we had, we had legal custody of her. He looked over the documents and they seemed to check out. Anna assured him that the Director from Mexico lied, he knew exactly where we were, how else could he have found us. The Immigration Officer left us, and the adoption was finalized. Her birth name was Candy and through the adoption we changed it to Sandra, nicknaming her Sandy. Our little miracle baby girl belonged to us, making an even dozen.

CHAPTER 14
ON THE MOVE

HUNGERFORD, TEXAS

I realized this was the end of our Missionary work in Mexico. Our Flame of Truth Board of Directors had a meeting, to decide where we go from here. We all agreed God has given us many gifts and talents, and we needed to find another place to open a Bible College in the states. There were some talented teachers in our group that wanted to be a part of it, and I had some experience teaching Spanish classes that were very successful. We were all in.

Several churches from Houston, TX were planning to partner with us, so we started to look for a property somewhere near Houston. We came across an empty Public School building near Hungerford, Texas which was selling on sealed bids. Several of the Board Members decided on a price, the sealed bids were opened. The local School Board said that the bids were too low, ours was the highest. One of their School Board Members asked us what we planned to use these buildings for. We told them that we were going to use the buildings for a Bible Training Center as well as a Drug and Alcohol Rehabilitation Center. They met together and decided to accept our bid as is. Everyone agreed that it was time to move our family to Hungerford, TX. God worked out all the details. One of the families from Houston had a mobile home and they no longer needed it. We transferred the deed and had a home to move our family into. At this point most of the older children had graduated from High School, and as they graduated, they moved back home to Pennsylvania, so we were now a family of seven.

When we arrived at the school, I was discouraged, I made up my mind that I was never going back to Mexico. I gave all the papers from Flame of Truth to our Board Members. I gave them the Charter as well as the deeds for the properties we had in San Juan, Texas. I was burned to the core and never wanted to see Mexico again.

The school building was vacant for years and was in major need of repair. We were put in charge of the building repair, making sure the school was ready by the end of the summer for grand opening in the fall.

I set up one room for Spanish classes. God gave me the knowledge to set up a Spanish lab. I was able to play prior recordings to all the students on head phones. I had it set up electronically, so I could listen to their pronunciation as they were instructed to repeat phrases. I could instruct all the students at the same time, or I could instruct them individually. I had a total of 12 students in my class. To this day there are still four of the students on the Mission Field, speaking Spanish as if they were born in a Latin Country.

One year later, a local Assembly of God Church we were associated with in Hungerford Texas, and another church nearby invited us to join them for revival meetings. One night after the meeting the pastor invited the Evangelist and my family to their home for fellowship. I shared with them the great things God was doing at the Bible College. After mentioning the name of some of the leaders, the Evangelist's wife asked me to please greet the President for her. The next morning, I visited the President's office. I told him someone at the revival asked me to greet you on their behalf. He asked who it was, and when I told him, he looked at me sternly and asked what she said about him. I told him she said nothing, only to give you her greetings. He got very angry with me, he treated me as if I was hiding something from him. I went to the Dean of the College confused and asked why the President would be so angry with me, he told me that he would do his best to try and find out. I discovered, without realizing, I had exposed something big that the President, the Board Members and the local Pastors did not want anyone to know about.

Several days later I was ordered to come to a meeting in Houston. When I arrived at the meeting, all the Board Members were present. I was threatened and was asked to leave. They told me that I was finished at the Bible College as of that day. They gave me thirty days to vacate and remove our mobile home from the property. I still did not know what was going on, but I knew it was something I did not want to be a part of.

I told them that they needed to return everything I brought with me, including all the documents for Flame of Truth, the mailing list, and the deeds of the two properties in San Juan. They refused to comply, they ordered me to leave. One of the Board Members was a business man who was my best friend for many years. He invested in Flame of Truth, in Mexico and here at the College. He encouraged them to give me what I brought to the table, they finally agreed and sent me packing.

During this time the dishonest man that used to be our Native Director of the Churches and Bible School in Mexico contacted me about the Bible School property. He told me that he had a buyer for the property. He told me that soon after we closed the Bible School, a bus was traveling on the highway and suddenly the steering broke and the bus came across the parking lot of the school and hit the wall in the middle of the chapel. In Mexico, they tie all four walls together at the top with concrete and steel rebar. The bus went in one side of the building and out the other. It caught the ring at the top of the building as it went through pulling all four walls down. So now the whole Chapel was destroyed, only the dormitories were left. The property was almost a total loss. I could not go back to Mexico, so we agreed to sell the property for a third of what we spent on it. Later we discovered that the dishonest Director had already sold the roof and pocketed the money. Everything was gone.

I still had a big problem. I did not want to go back to Mexico, there was no Bible School or Orphanage to go back to, everything was gone. Now what will I do? Here I am at a cross road again, which way do I go? We realized that we had to go back to San Juan, we at least had a house to go back to and we would have to trust God to figure out the rest.

We sent a letter to all the Flame of Truth supporters explaining that we were no longer affiliated with the school. We discovered from some of our supporters that the Christian Brotherhood Foundation board kept soliciting them for funds long after we were gone. It was obvious the Board kept a copy of the Flame of Truth supporters addresses for themselves. With the Flame of Truth supporters gone, the school ended up closing the doors. God can open the doors and He can close them as He sees fit.

Today those buildings serve as a rehabilitation center for Teen Challenge. Thank God, it was not all lost.

CHAPTER 15
BACK TO SAN JUAN, TEXAS

FLYING TO GUATEMALA

Now back in San Juan, Texas, trying to figure out where God was leading us next. I looked back, and I realized that God knew our future and was already opening the doors for what he had in store for the Ministry. While I was still teaching Spanish at the Bible College in Hungerford, TX, a friend of mine from Florida decided to move to the school to help with the Missionary work. He was a pilot and owned his own airplane. We planned on flying into Central America supporting the missionaries and pastors. We made our first trip to Guatemala. Since my friend's airplane was a high-performance plane, it was not possible to land at the jungle runway, it was way too short for his plane. We had to land at an airstrip in Sayaxché and travel the rest of the way on boat, about a half day ride down river.

When we arrived at the Mission, we jumped right in helping with whatever needed to be done. The power plant equipment was neglected and in need of repair. Supplies were hard to come by. There was no Lowes or Home Depot around the corner. They had to travel down the river half a day. It was too dangerous on the river after dark, so if it got too late in the day, they could not return until the following morning. The cost of materials was expensive, even the cost for fuel was more than three times the price of fuel in the US. In two days, I had the power plant operating like new.

The friend from Florida moved with us from Hungerford, to San Juan Texas, and the airplane trips to Guatemala continued. Another trip to Guatemala, we started a teaching seminar in the day time at the Mission, in the evening we went to different services up and down the river by boat.

I remember in one of the villages after service it was too late to return to the Mission, so we had to stay overnight. The villagers told us that it was very dangerous for us to stay there that night. They told us that the local school teacher was a member of a vigilante group, and they came over from Mexico threatening the villagers, that the military was coming to kill them, so many of the villagers were fleeing overnight. We had to stay, so we stacked most of the church benches up against the door, blocking the entrance so that if they came to get us, they would at least have to wake us up. That way we could at least rebuke them in the name of Jesus, we knew there is power in His name. We stayed awake and prayed most of the night. At daylight, we were able to get in our boat and return to the Mission. Thank God, nothing happened.

On our return trip in the plane, we flew into a severe rain storm. It rained so hard we could barely recognize where we were. We decided to try and land at an airstrip along the coast. When we located the village, it rained so hard that we lost all visibility and could not see the airstrip. The flood water had covered the ground, it was too dangerous for us to land, but we had gone too far to turn back. The pilot was a very experienced pilot as he was a former Crop Duster Pilot for many years. He decided to head for Texas, and he said by the time we get to McAllen, TX, there will be a hole in the sky. Otherwise we will find an airport somewhere nearby. He headed the plane in that direction. Soon he told me I needed to fly the plane, he needed to get on the radio and cross reference our path from radio station to radio station, to figure out where we are. That was the only means of navigation we had in those days for small airplanes. This was before the days of GPS. About every five minutes he showed me on the map exactly where we were flying. Several times we hit severe turbulences where he would take over the controls because I had no experience in flying an airplane. Sometimes you could see the wing of the plane light up during a lightning strike nearby. Sometimes you could see nothing but a heavy cloud covering the plane. He told me that we need not worry about a lightning strike, as the airplane was not grounded, it will not harm us. About twenty miles out of McAllen we came out of the storm and a hole opened in the clouds just as my friend believed would happen. Thank God we were able to land safely. What a stressful trip, it was great to have our feet on the ground.

Soon after this trip my friend decided to move back to Florida. He told me that we both don't need to be flying to Central America. He told me if I would like to learn to fly an airplane, he would like to pay for my flight training, I then can purchase an airplane more suitable for jungle flying than his. I started taking lessons and soon I was ready for the flight test and passed. Now I was ready for our first airplane.

Meanwhile I had met another man that he and his wife were pilot instructors. They had purchased a Cesna 182, a perfect plane for the jungles. We flew together to Guatemala. When we arrived there, we flew over the landing strip to check it out. As you may imagine, in the jungle you may encounter some problems, there may be cattle or even pigs on the airstrip, all looked well. The pilot made the last turn for the final landing. He was coming way too fast for the short runway. He hit the ground so hard that the plane bounced at least ten feet in the air. I yelled for him to pull up and make another attempt, I knew the strip was way too short. He decided to set it down anyways. We got near the end of the runway, still traveling at about thirty miles per hour, we knew we were in trouble. The pilot was able to do what we call a ground loop. The plane did a 180 turn, by doing this he was able to stop the plane with the power of the engine. He had never flown into the jungles before and soon learned that there is a vast difference in the dry hot jungles or on a paved runway in the US. He decided jungle flying was not for him.

PURCHASING AN AIRPLANE

Through a pilot friend of ours in Missouri we found an Aero Commander Darter for sale, a great little plane. Our Board Members agreed that it was time to buy one of our own. Since we now had the money from the sale of the Bible School property we decided to purchase it.

Aero Commander Darter

This was the beginning of my jungle flying. I made my first trip into Guatemala in the Darter with two men from Williamsport PA. I soon realized that this plane was too underpowered to fly into the short air strips of the jungle, so we landed in Sayaxché in the Petén Jungles. Then we needed to take another long boat ride to La Anchura.

When we arrived at the Mission, we began to make plans for the week. We were teaching in the day time at the Mission, in the evening we ministered to the churches up and down the river.

When it came time to leave for home, we first had that long boat ride back to Sayaxché where the plane was parked. The weather was very hot that day and I was concerned about liftoff. I learned when the weather is very hot the engine does not have as much power as in cooler temperatures. Neither does the wing have as much lifting affect. I walked down the runway to check things out. I marked a place on the ground, where we must be off the ground, or we will not clear the trees and will have to abort takeoff. We loaded our things in the plane, started the engine and got ready for takeoff. We headed down the runway hoping that we would have enough lift/power by the marked point. When we arrived at the point we did not have enough speed for takeoff. I shut the engine down and returned to the starting point. We got out and began to pray. Dear God, please help us in our situation. Suddenly a cloud covered the area, I yelled for the brothers to jump in quickly. The coolness of the cloud and a bit of wind blowing was all we needed for takeoff.

Coming back from that trip I asked God for a better plane because this one is too dangerous to continue to fly into the jungles. I heard there was a Cesna 182 for sale that a Missionary had used in Mexico. It was the perfect plane built for jungle flying, it was more equipped for short take-off and landings. We were able to trade in the Dart and from the money that our supporters provided, we were able to buy the Cesna 182 plane.

Cesna 182

FLYING TO HONDURAS

I soon learned to be a jungle pilot. I started making trips to Honduras nearly every month. I worked with a doctor in Honduras and became very efficient in the medical practice.

Two other Missionary Pilots and I were asked to move a missionary family to Wampusirpe, near the West Coast in the jungles of Honduras. The family was going to Honduras to start a Bible School. We all flew close to each other. The husband flew with me and the wife and their daughter flew with the second plane. The third plane was carrying the family's personal belongings. On our way, we encountered some bad weather. The cloud cover was so thick, visibility was zero. We were sure by the time we arrived on the East Coast there would be an opening in the clouds to come down. So, we decided to go up through the clouds. Suddenly the pilot carrying the two ladies, radioed an emergency call. He began to yell, "I lost control, my plane is upside down, No, now I am right side up, but I am in a spiral." We were trained for these types of emergencies, but the Pilot was in panic mode. I told him to push the wheel all the way in to the firewall and it will come out of the spiral. We were still in the thick clouds and I knew he was in front of me, but I did not know how soon I might catch up to him. To prevent a collision, I decided to go down below the clouds, so I could see him coming. The husband heard all of this going on and feared for his family's lives. We began to pray and watched for them to come out of the clouds, but we could not see them anywhere. It was not much longer, the pilot radioed back, thanking God they were ok.

I was so shook-up, that I landed at the closest airport. It was not much longer, that the pilot radioed back and told me that he was out of the clouds and can see the East Coast. I took off immediately to join the other two. I didn't see them again until we landed in the airport in Chetumal near Belize. Quite a crazy experience.

We stayed there for the night. Next day we flew over Belize to Honduras. We headed for the jungles on the West Coast. This part of the trip went smoothly. We located the air strip in Wampusirpe. One of the other pilots landed first, it was decided that I land next. I came in very slow and only used a short section of the airstrip. My plane had a STOL kit installed. Stands for (Short take-off and landing) I could land at a much slower speed than without it.

I warned the third pilot to come in as slow as possible. He came down on the airstrip way too fast for conditions. He ran past the end of the airstrip, continued into a trail in the jungle. He followed it until he was able to come to a complete stop. I asked him why he came in so fast, and did not follow instruction, he told me that I made it look so easy when I landed, so he came in at normal speed. No one was hurt, and we thanked God that the trail was there preventing damage to the plane. He could have crashed into the trees and the outcome would have been a lot worse. If you don't learn quickly, the jungle will eat you up.

The couple started a Bible School and trained many local ministers for the work in Honduras They built a home and lived there for several years. They trained some local leaders to run the Mission on their own. They felt it was time to move back to the US, they completed their mission. We picked them up again and brought them back to Texas.

I made many trips to Honduras. Taught in many seminars. I was asked to serve on the Gospel Crusade Ministerial Fellowship (GCMF) Board of Honduras for several years. I made some difficult trips into Honduras, sometimes solo, ministering and spreading the Gospel of Jesus Christ.

On one trip I was asked by the doctor I was working with, to hold a clinic in Puerto Lempira. He said he scheduled a clinic there, but something came up and he could not go. He instructed me to completely refer to the book "Where There Is No Doctor", for instructions on treating the illnesses and trusted me to know my limits.

A small child came to the clinic dangerously dehydrated. I was able to save her life by giving her an oral IV solution over night until we were able to get her to a hospital the next day.

Pastor asked me to go to another village to hold a clinic there as well. There I found a woman that just gave birth 18-days prior where both the mother and the baby had a severe case of Malaria. I took them back to the clinic with me and the next day I flew them to another village in the jungle where there was a clinic with a doctor. I stayed there with them and paid for the blood transfusion for the mother and medicine for the baby. After treatment, I flew them back to their village.

There was a Convention going on that weekend, Sunday night after the Convention was over I had people come to the clinic with all kinds of medical needs. At about mid-night two men came in from the jungle for parasite treatments. Before I gave them anything I led both to the Lord Jesus Christ. After the two men left, The Director of Missions was there watching and came to me. He said we need a clinic here, He told me that God laid it on his heart while I was treating those men to fund it. Soon after that they began construction on the clinic. They now have a clinic operating there twenty-four hours a day with full staff. Glory to God.

One day while I was helping at the clinic, I was asked to go to the lady's dormitory because a lady was having attacks. I asked for a lady I knew well to accompany me. When I arrived, the lady's family was trying to help her. I soon realized that it was not a medical issue, she was demon possessed and needed deliverance. When she had an attack, her family would splash alcohol in her face. As I was praying for her deliverance, the family would continue to interrupt and pour alcohol on her, every time she had another attack, and everything would get worse. I prayed and asked Jesus to help me. God helped me to see that the family was hindering her from deliverance and God spoke to me to tell everybody to leave the room except the lady I invited with me. Her family did not want to leave. I asked them if they want their sister to be delivered, they must give her to God. I told them, when they leave, she will be delivered. They left the room and in just a few minutes she was delivered from demon possession. In most countries they do not know what to do with a demon possessed person and put them in a mental institution or a hospital. In Latin America we have them delivered by the power of God.

I flew all over the jungles of Honduras. Landed in many jungle strips. Including Roatan Island. Taught in many conferences. Helped in many places in the clinics. Carried ministers by plane to other conferences.

I thank God for letting me be an instrument in his hands doing whatever He wants me to do and go where He needs me to go for his honor and glory.

MISSIONARY DOCTOR

Our Missionary Doctor, Dr. José Angel Reyna is a Mexican National, who also serves as President of Flama de la Verdad. He is a great preacher of the Gospel of Jesus Christ. He and his wife Nora have been working with us for over 25 years. He is a man with great respect and character.

Dr. Reyna is my right-hand man in Mexico today. He has taken my place in many situations. If I need anything done in Mexico, he is the man that gets it done. He is a full-fledged licensed Medical Doctor in Mexico that gave up his entire medical career, to be a full time Missionary Doctor. Taking care of the people that cannot afford healthcare. He has clinics all over Mexico in church buildings or wherever the doors open for him. Flame of Truth supporters purchased land and built a clinic for him in Reynosa, Mexico.

Flame of Truth was also able to buy a Mobile Clinic for him through the supporters, that can get him into places that he could not get into before. It has served the medical profession in many areas. A hurricane hit the State of Chiapas Mexico. A friend of ours from North Carolina drove the Mobile Clinic down for us. The local doctors there had no place to take care of their patients due to the hurricane flooding. It served the Missionary Doctor and the local doctors until they were able to rebuild.

Dr Reyna also oversees the distribution of the Food Program, "Kids against Hunger" all over Mexico. The food comes in cases of 32 packets which feeds 6 people per packet, a total of 192 meals. It comes to us by tractor trailer load, free of charge. Wow, what a blessing. We store the load and take it into Mexico as needed. We also have other Missionaries and Mexican Pastors that come and pick it up for their communities. Dr Reyna takes food to areas that suffer major disaster in Mexico. He delivered several loads of food and tents to Juchitan, Oaxaca after a major earth-quake.

Dr Reyna is a great preacher of the Word of God

Please pray for him, his wife Nora and his family, that God continues to provide funds for him to continue to do what he does in Jesus name. When you pray for him, you are praying for me and my Ministry. Without him I would be limited as to what I could do in Mexico because of the International Laws.

CHAPTER 16
INSTITUTE OF MINISTRY FLIGHTS

IOM IN HONDURAS

Gospel Crusade Ministerial Fellowship (GCMF) started the "Institutes of Ministries" (IOM) under the direction of Gerald Derstine from Bradenton, Florida. It was a Bible Seminar on "Victorious Christian Living". I flew to Tegucigalpa, Honduras to help with the first classes and soon became the Assistant Director. I taught a class as well as interpreted for several other teachers. The Institute had a tremendous impact on the people's lives.

One weekend after the IOM classes, the local pastors asked me to drive the church van to visit a church in the North Eastern part of Honduras, not far from the Guatemala border. We drove and drove and for some reason we didn't get there until about ten-thirty that night, a nine-and-a-half-hour trip. There were no issues on the trip to delay us, according to the pastor we should have been there around seven or eight pm. When we arrived, the pastor told us that the people are still in the church waiting for us to preach. I could not believe that they would wait this late. He told me I can preach later, I had to eat first. So, they quickly killed several chickens, and put them in the pot to cook. I suggested that I could preach while the food was cooking and eat later. He told me the people don't mind waiting. They insisted I take care of my physical needs first.

At midnight we started to preach. The people were so hungry for the word, they just drew it out of me. I never experienced this hunger for the Word in the US. The service ended around two o'clock in the morning.

Early the next morning we woke to the people preparing food for breakfast. We got up and washed up with a bucket of cold water. When we finished breakfast, the people were waiting for us in the church for us to preach to them again. The pastor told me that there is not enough room for everyone in the church building, so one of the young ladies and himself took the children outside and taught them a Sunday School lesson while I preached. I taught on the Baptism of the Holy Spirit that morning. I was near the end of the teaching, when the pastor came running inside all excited and interrupted the sermon. He announced that all the children are receiving the Baptism of the Holy Spirit outside and asked what he should do. I thought for a moment, I knew there was no room anywhere in the church building except on the platform. I told him to bring them to me. As I was giving the alter call for the adults, I was led to have the children lay hands on the adults. When they did, a marvelous thing happened. The adults were also being filled with the Holy Spirit all over the place. It seemed like the day of Pentecost.

Somehow, on our return trip to Tegucigalpa, we made it back in seven hours. To this day I still do not understand why it took us so long to get to that village the day before. All I can say is that God sometimes has other things in mind to bring us surprises. I will never forget that trip or those people who touched my heart and soul.

IOM in Honduras

IOM IN GUATEMALA

One of the other IOM conferences was in Guatemala. I remember one Sunday night, when there were no classes scheduled, I decided to visit a local church. I sat respectfully in the service as the pastor ministered. Suddenly, a lady got up and began to prophesy. Her prophesy was, "God says that everyone in this church is living in sin, everyone. No one is in right standing with God, no one." I thought for a bit about what she said, I knew I was in right standing with God. Sometimes God uses me in the gift of prophesy as well as the gift of knowledge, and discernment. I knew in my spirit that this was not a word from God. I heard someone say that she was their prophetess. Since I was in someone else's church I had great respect for the pastor. So, I waited until everyone was gone and approached him. I asked the pastor if he was in right standing with God? He said, "I sure am." I told him, "not according to that lady that prophesied. Not only you. But she said me also. I know that I am in right standing with God. According to her own words, that makes her a false prophet." I reminded him that she said "everyone". The pastor was ashamed, because they thought she was a real prophet. He was so glad that I discerned her spirit and made him realize that she really did prophesy falsely. He told me that she will no longer be the prophetess in this church.

IOM IN COLUMBIA

I was asked to go to Columbia to help oversee the IOM there. The IOM was a real success. That weekend, I was asked to fly to a city to minister to the people in one of the churches there. I felt led to teach on Home Relations.

Knowing the Latin Culture, I decided to do something special. After I was finished teaching, I told them that many people are ashamed to kiss their wife in public places. I told them that I still open the car door for my wife when we go somewhere and when I do, I always hug and kiss her, she is my wife and I have a license to do so. It doesn't matter where we are. Obviously, I am very respectful, keeping it rated G. I said it is time that we get rid of our pride and treat our wives as we treated them when we were first married. My children knew that I loved my wife and I also hug and kiss our children. I apologized for my wife not being there with me, so I could show them how it is done.

I asked for a couple to volunteer and asked them to come to the platform and help me. I asked them to be an example in my place since Anna is not here. I asked the husband to remember how he loved his wife when they were first married. I reminded him that he didn't care who saw them back then. They hugged and kissed before the congregation. Soon all the couples followed suit. There was so much true love flowing in that place. Everyone thanked me for helping them realize how they took each other for granted and were slacking. I encouraged everyone to always turn to their own spouse for love and affection, then they will not have so many temptations when they see lustful people in the world. I encouraged them to enjoy their marriage to the fullest, then their life will be full of great pleasure and enjoyment.

A lady once told me a story. There was a couple, when they were first married, that went to the City Park. It was a beautiful moon lit night. The wife looked at the moon and asked, "what is that up there that shines so beautifully?" The husband replied, "don't you know honey, that is the moon that shines so beautifully to enhance our love as we sit here together so lovingly." After they were married five years they happened to sit on the same park bench. The moon again was so bright. The wife asked her husband the same question as she did five years previously. "What is that up there that shines so beautifully?" The husband replied, "Stupid, don't you know it is the moon."

She went right into another story. She told me that another couple when they were first married were going to town on the bus. The wife slipped and began to fall. The husband grabbed her and said, "be careful honey you could fall and break a leg or something." She was so grateful. Five years after they were married they were going to town on the bus, the wife slipped and began to fall, the husband left her fall. He said, "get up stupid, can't you walk on your own two feet." That is what happens over time, when you get comfortable and let your love light go out.

IOM in Columbia

IOM IN COSTA RICA

I flew to Costa Rica for the IOM. I arrived there two days before any other teachers to prepare for the classes. The church people asked me where I was from. I told them that I was from the United States. They said that they couldn't believe me because my Spanish was so perfect. How can

an American speak such good Spanish? They told me I
speak fluent Spanish with a perfect accent and I sound like I
was from the capital of Mexico City.

The third day I was there, I was asked to take the church
van and pick up the GCMF leaders at the airport. As I was
talking to the leaders in English, the local people heard me
and were shocked that I could speak English so well. I was
able to share with them how God gave me the gift of the
Spanish language in prayer one day. I told them that only
God can help you perfect any language that you were not
born with. You will always have your native accent when you
speak another language, the new language accent is nearly
impossible to perfect without God.

IOM in Costa Rica

IOM IN MEXICO

We were invited back to Uruapan MX, I flew down to set
up and I heard there were too many people registered to
hold the conference in the same building we were in the first
year, so the church rented an auditorium. I am sure there
were more than two hundred fifty people registered. One
night I was teaching on the Holy Ghost. When I invited the
people to come forward to receive the Holy Ghost. The

anointing of God fell on the place in a very unusual way. I was sure that night at least one hundred and twenty people received the Holy Ghost. Another day of Pentecost. It happened so fast that we could not even begin to count them.

IOM in Mexico

IOM IN ARGENTINA.

I spent two weeks in Argentina, approximately 20 years ago. It was a glorious experience. I had a marvelous time teaching mostly young people. I taught on how the youth needed to be involved in Ministry. I remember one day I rolled up a piece of paper with a string sticking out of the top, it looked like a real stick of dynamite if I must say so myself. During the teaching I asked for a young man and a young lady volunteer. I gave the so-called stick of dynamite to the young lady and I gave a pack of matches to the young man. I said this is an example of what happens to our young people when they operate carnally and not under Christian principles. I instructed the young man to take the matches and light the fuse of the dynamite. Of course, they flatly refused to cooperate as they both thought that it really was a stick of dynamite. I assured them that it was not real, it was only an example. I shared how taking a relationship too far can result in destroying the relationship, unwanted pregnancies, and all kinds of problems.

A young man that attended the IOM kept asking me if it were possible for him to travel with me just to carry my briefcase. His desire was to have the anointing I have. I told him that it was not necessary for him to travel with me, if he wanted what I had. I can pray for him and the same anointing that he feels is upon me, he can have as well. I laid my hands on him and prayed. I asked God to anoint him with that same anointing.

I didn't hear from anyone from Argentina for a number of years. Someone came to me in Pennsylvania at a Missionary Conference and asked if I was in Argentina. I assured him that I was. He asked me if I remembered a young man that asked me to pray for him to receive the same anointing I had. He told me that not long ago there was a Nationwide Revival in Argentina, and that same young man was one of the four leaders in that revival. God's anointing was all over him and he was preaching the Gospel. You may never know what legacy you may pass on to others, when you let God use you for his honor and glory.

IOM in Argentina

IOM IN HAITI

I received a call to go to the Island of Haiti for the IOM to teach on "Home Relations". I told the Lord that I needed a miracle, I needed twenty-seven hundred dollars for my plane ticket. I got an invitation to minister in two churches in Texas and I was hoping to raise the funds to pay for the trip.

I arrived in the church in Midland, Texas, five hundred miles away from home. The pastor told me they had a church split and are thinking about closing the church doors. He told me that he was sorry he could not help the ministry more because, the offerings are little to nothing. I ministered that night, and the offering was around thirty dollars. I went to bed in the motor home that night, parked in the church parking lot. I asked God how I will be able to fly to Haiti without the funds. Around twelve o'clock someone knocked on my door. I heard a lady's voice telling me that God told her to bring this to me. I wasn't sure whether it was appropriate to answer the door for a lady that late at night. I opened the door a little as I was not completely dressed. She handed me an envelope and said God bless you. I opened the envelope and began to count one hundred-dollar bills. Guess how many there were? You guessed it twenty-seven one hundred-dollar bills. I mentioned in the service that I needed to go to Haiti, but I had not shared the amount of funds needed for the trip. God knew and did the math!!

The second church was around two hundred miles away where I was scheduled to go to in Del Rio, TX. When I arrived there, I had another surprise. The pastor had forgotten that I was coming, and he was in the middle of a week revival with another Evangelist. He apologized, and I headed home with the blessing of the Lord and was able to purchase my ticket to go to Haiti.

When I arrived in Haiti, we started our two-week classes. The people responded very well. They asked me many questions, and I answered them to the best of my ability and of course what the Bible has to say about the subject. Sunday morning, the pastor asked me to minister to his large congregation. After the service, the pastor told me that six couples wanted me to join them for lunch. He told me they had many questions about how they can continue teaching the people like I did. When I arrived at the house they all told me that during the two-week course, when I was teaching, the Lord spoke to their heart to continue doing what I was doing. I shared my wisdom and my material as well as instructions as best I knew how. I prayed for the anointing of God that was on me to be upon them.

Four years ago, I asked the Director of GCMF how the six couples were doing in Haiti. He assured me that all six couples were still working with the married couples in the church. They are doing a great job helping them keep the victory in their marriages. As I said before, you may never realize the legacy you leave behind wherever you go. It doesn't matter what you feel when you are ministering. You may not think that you are getting the message across the way you wanted to. What really matters is that God can take what you say and do what he wants to with it. All you can do, is do the best you can, and God does the rest. God can use anyone that will allow Him, just so we give Him the honor and the glory. Without Him we would be a complete failure.

VIDEO INSTITUTE OF MINISTRIES (VIOM)

Requests from churches to host the IOM classes was coming in from all over Mexico, Central America, South America and even in the US. It became very clear that one man could not be at every place at the same time. The first year of conferences, a friend recorded all the classes in the IOM in Uruapan, Michoacán, Mexico, and we realized that we had a video library started. The following year, I learned to use the video camera and we recorded the two-week classes, four, 2-hour sessions daily, approximately one hundred hours of teaching, making all the new teachings available to more churches through video. So, the VIOM was born.

I wish I would have kept count of all the sets of VHS tapes I duplicated, it was extensive. I am sure that there are well over three hundred, plus sets distributed. We always provided the cassette player for the participating church along with the VHS videos then the church needed to provide the TV for the classes. When the church was finished with the VIOM, they were expected to pass it on to a student in attendance to share the gospel of Jesus with their village. Each set was used repeatedly.

The whole set was an apple box of 50 VHS cassettes plus the player. Years later, we added 28 more hours to the set, 128 hours of teaching the Word of God and his principles of Victorious Christian Living. With new technology, we now have them available on DVD and fit in a folder of 32 DVD's.

50 VHS tapes = I apple box full

Now 128 hrs.   *A 32-disk folder. Held
in 1 hand*

Pastor Rodrigo Medonado from Santa Catarina, Nuevo Leon near Monterey has been our Representative for the VIOM Schools all over Mexico as well as several in the US. Our supporters for Flame of Truth, are able to be missionaries and win souls for Christ without leaving home. They can sponsor churches for a fifty-dollar donation, plus delivery costs to provide the VIOM program. Teaching their congregation, and communities how to live a victorious life in Jesus Christ and train others.

The VIOM Representative informed me that in the State of Chiapas Mexico, they were hosting a VIOM with thirty-six Students. Twenty-four of the students were pastors. He said that the class of thirty-six students were watching the video classes on a little four-inch TV. I cannot imagine thirty-six students huddling around to watch a teaching video on a little TV like that and getting that much out of it. The pastors were so excited about the VIOM that they disputed over which one would be chosen to take the classes to their village first. Again, these people were so hungry for the teaching of the Word of God.

According to the new laws in Mexico, pastors are required to be certified through some Bible School course. VIOM is a Government approved certified course. For this reason, there is still a demand for them today.

CHAPTER 17
THE MINISTRY TODAY

HAPPY ANNIVERSARY

In August of 1998, our children helped us celebrate our 50th Wedding Anniversary. They planned a beautiful wedding, that Anna always dreamed of, but never had due to our circumstances. We renewed our vows with our twelve children as the Wedding Party and our thirty-seven living Grand Children as the Ring Bearers and Flower Girls. All twelve of our children were at the same place at the same time, which is a feat, since they are spread out from Texas to Pennsylvania and Michigan. We were so blessed. We are now ready to celebrate our Seventieth Wedding Anniversary on September 25th, 2018.

On January 7, 2018, we celebrated the Fifty-fifth-year Anniversary of Flame of Truth Ministry. God has been so good and faithful to us. It has been a roller coaster ride, and it is great to see how God prepared the track in front of us and kept us on track and never left us down.

HOME BASE MINISTRY

During the last 34 years we have been building a home base for missionaries to help meet all their needs. We purchased ten acres of land near Donna, Texas. On the east side of the property we had 1300 feet of runway. I was able to fly to Mexico and the jungles of Central America right from my back yard.

Years later, the neighbors built a house across the road right in front of the airstrip, making it too dangerous to land and takeoff. At the same time my health began to deteriorate, and the maintenance of the plane became too costly to continue. We had to sell the airplane, however, it is still being used for missions near the North Pole. It seemed like the Lord was closing that chapter of my life. God has everything under control.

We started to focus on helping and meeting the needs of other missionaries. The airstrip became a campground to give the missionaries a place to stay while renewing their Visas bi-annually and replenishing their supplies in the US. It is not for profit for vacationers or Winter Texans. The campground is also used for groups from the US coming to help missionaries in their projects. We are fifteen minutes from the border of Mexico, making it easy for the groups to go to Mexico in the daytime to work with the missions and come back to the US in the evening to shower and sleep in air-conditioned dormitories or trailers at night.

For years, our second son, Mervin was the mechanic on the Home Base and would repair the Missionary's vehicles at cost. Currently we do not have a full-time mechanic. Our son-in-law Richard uses the garage to maintain our vehicles and equipment and occasionally helps with other missionary vehicle repairs.

We also handle mailing for some missionaries as well as their finances. Some Mexican pastors receive support from the US, so we handle the mail as it comes in and we do the banking for them, providing a tax-exempt receipt for the donor.

We have a Food Pantry to meet the physical needs of the missionaries and the local people. Every other Tuesday morning, we provide spiritual food as well as physical. The local people register and join us for a Bible Study and we provide them with food for their families. There is very little donations from local businesses, but with the donations from our supporters we can purchase food for pennies on the dollar from a Food Bank Distribution Center.

We have a church on the property that our daughter, Linda and her husband Richard pastor, with Sunday services and a Tuesday evening Bible Study. A local Spanish Church uses the facilities every Sunday afternoon. The church building is available for groups to use by appointment when it is not in use.

THE MISSIONFIELD

We are still on the Mission Field. Over the years, I have ministered in 13 different countries, including the United States, Canada, Mexico, Belize, Guatemala, Honduras, Nicaragua, Costa Rica, Columbia, Argentina, Haiti, Dominican Republic & Puerto Rico.

Our oldest daughter Linda had been talking to her husband Richard for years about moving from their home in Missouri and helping Mother and Father in the Texas & Mexico Ministry. Richard told her that if he ever went to the mission field it would be to China. On their way home to Missouri after a visit with us in Texas, Richard asked Linda, if she was ready to move. She asked him not to tease her like that, and he told her that he was serious. He said, "if that is where God wants us, then I am ready to move." They started making plans for the move. They put their house up for sale. It was not long, a couple came by and said this is the house they wanted for a long time and bought it. In January 1999 they moved to Texas. They said they were coming to take care of Mother & Father while they are aging and after they are gone they will take over the Mission work. They have taken over most of the responsibilities for Flame of Truth as I am writing this book. Linda and Richard have jumped right in as if they were made for It. They pastor the Light House Church here on the campus. Linda is doing most of the managing around here on the Missionary Home Base. She does most of the office work, which keeps her very busy. She manages the Food Pantry for the local people as well as for the Missionaries. Every summer she writes and organizes the programs for Vacation Bible School's in Texas as well as in Mexico. Her husband Richard is kept busy doing maintenance, preaching, making mission trips into Mexico, and assisting in anything he can do to help on the Home Base.

Our son Victor and wife Angie also moved onto the Home Base to help with the ministry. Besides operating his own construction business, he helps extensively in the church as well as helping to maintain the RV trailers in the park and the buildings on the property. He is our emergency trouble shooter and repair man, jack of all trades.

Victor is also a trained Security Guard, on occasion he has had to defend and detain thieves on the property. He is there for us day or night. We are blessed to have him and his wife by our side. Linda and Victor are doing such a mighty work for the Lord. Carrying the torch and passing on my legacy.

The work in Mexico is doing great. One of our pastors Rosendo Garcia from Charco Azul recently told Linda, "Brother High taught us how to do mission work and now it is our responsibility to carry on the legacy." He started branching out and spreading the Gospel. He traveled to a place called Wichiwayan, in the state of San Louise Potosí, close to Tampico, about five hundred miles south of the border. He is now working with five pastors there. Together with our daughter, her husband and the local people, they helped build a new Church in El Cañon which was dedicated in July 2017.

CHAPTER 18
GOD'S CONTINUING HEALING POWER

MY HEALTH

Satan tried thirteen times since childhood to take my life and he failed every time. God had a plan, and he is not finished with me.

My health started really declining in 1998 and 1999. My knees were beginning to cause me a lot of pain. In December of 1999 I had both knees replaced. As I was regaining my strength and mobility back. Things were seemingly getting back to normal. The knee replacements lasted quite a while. I had one replaced recently and need to schedule the second replacement the end of 2018.

On December 16, 2000, we were having a Men's Prayer Breakfast, when suddenly I started feeling chest pains. I recalled my heart attack when I was thirty in the Mennonite Church. I remembered the pain was so severe then, but it was not close to feeling the same this time, so I thought it must be indigestion. I felt like this, many times before, I would drink water, or a soda pop and it would go away. This time it would not go away, it kept getting a bit stronger.

Our youngest son Victor was sitting next to me. He looked at me and asked if I was ok. I told him that I was having indigestion. He told me that I didn't look good and thought he should take me to a doctor. I finally agreed to go, and he took me to the local hospital. They checked me out, and after tests, the doctor came back and told me I was having a heart attack. They did the procedures necessary to stop it. The doctor came back and told us that the report was not too good, and he was scheduling me for a Triple bypass surgery in the morning. Dec. 17, 2000, on Sunday morning, on Anna's birthday. They took me to the operating room. I was not too concerned, I thought it was no big deal, I felt fine. When I came out of anesthesia, I had tubes sticking out of my stomach, mouth and nose. The nurse assured me that I was ok and allowed Anna and our youngest adopted daughter Sandra to come in to see me. I did not recover very well from that surgery, I had no energy. It took me months to be able to do anything. I was disappointed in myself.

Sometime later, we were having a Missionary Fellowship Meeting. A friend of mine came to the meeting. He used to be just like I was with no energy, and now he was full of energy with some to spare. I asked him what he did to feel better. He told me that he started to take a special vitamin. I could not believe that a vitamin could make that much of a difference. He told me that is what he did, and it made him feel young again. I told him to sign me up. I started taking the same vitamins and in two weeks I started feeling like I had more energy and strength. I was soon able to go back to Mexico and preach the gospel again. My what a God we serve.

In 2001 my family Doctor. referred me to a Lung Specialist. They found out that I had Sleep Apnea. I stop breathing at night. Therefore, I was so tired and had headaches in the morning. Now I sleep with A CPAP machine, forcing air into my lungs and keeps me breathing.

DIAGNOSED WITH TERMINAL ILLNESS

In 2006 my lung Doctor talked me into getting the flu shot. In a short time, I was in the hospital with a severe lung infection, such as I have never experienced in my life. This re-occurred every four to six weeks for the next ten years.

One of the last times I was in the hospital I asked the Assistant Lung Specialist if there was anything they can give me to stop this infection from recurring. He looked at me straight in the eye and told me "they are doing everything they know how and told me this disease was terminal".

In 2016 the infections became less frequent. In 2017 I didn't have one serious lung infection. Again in 2018 I have not had a serious lung infection to date. The Lung Specialist did not change my treatment plan, I believe God is healing me or giving me new lungs. To God be the glory and all the praise.

Here I am in my Ninetieth-year, I am praying for my health and strength to continue to improve, so I can make more trips with Linda and Richard and our Mexico pastor, Missionary Doctor, Dr Reyna.

Anna and I continue to travel north to minister in the churches that support our ministry and raise funds for the mission work. Our bodies cannot stand the hot summer months here, so we travel from July and return early November in time for the holidays.

ANNA'S HEALTH

Anna has always been there for me through all my ailments. She has taken such good care of me and assisting me when I was down. Over the last year, her health has been deteriorating. She struggles with High Blood pressure, back pain, and weakness. Your continued prayers would be appreciated as we continue to do the work of the Lord. Living in the motor home for 4 months out of a year proves challenging on our bodies. We take one year at a time. Our children do not want us to take these trips alone, so our Son Clair is semi-retired and flies down to drive for us on the long trip up north. By the grace of God, we continue to itinerate and will continue as he deems so.

ANNA'S OUT OF BODY EXPERIENCE

We were invited to be a part of a weekend Conference in Monroe, Georgia. On Saturday afternoon they prepared a special meal with five or six different ethnic types of food. After we were finished eating, everyone was just fellowshipping around the tables. Anna said that she was not feeling very well, so I prayed a short prayer for her. Everything seemed to be ok. After a while I looked at her and realized something was not ok. I called out to her, but she did not respond. I saw something I had never seen before. She stared straight ahead, and her eyes looked so empty. I yelled for the other preachers to come help me pray, I believed she was gone. They prayed, we all prayed. Soon she started to move and looked at us confused as to what happened. She started to tell me that she was going way up above the room, looking down she could see everybody still sitting at the table, but we were getting smaller and smaller. Then suddenly, she was back, looking at us from her chair. I thank God that he gave me my wife back, and my life back because I would not want to live without her.

CHAPTER 19
I KNOW WHO HOLDS THE FUTURE

I am still resolved to follow God where ever he leads me. People keep telling me that God is not finished with me yet. I am not throwing in the towel, I know that God still has a work for me to do. I want to finish my course with great joy and when it is all over I expect to receive a great reward and crown in Heaven.

My desire is for each one of you to do as the Apostle Paul said, *follow me as I follow Christ*. I encourage you to believe that disappointments in life are not always as they seem. Usually God is working on our behalf to complete his will even better than what we ever thought possible. You can see in my life experiences, things did not seem to work out for the best for me. But you could also see how God had to close one door for the other to open. Sometimes, he had to slam the doors, but he was in control the whole time.

I pray God continues to use me to pray for the sick, as he has in the past. The miracles you read about in this book are absolutely by the power of God. My God is a big God. Only He can do that which you have read. All I had to do was give him my best, obey Him, and he did the rest. I give all the glory, honor and praise to Him. For without God I can do nothing. ***Jesus is the same yesterday, today and forever***.

CHAPTER 20
FLAME OF TRUTH

WHO WE ARE, WHAT WE DO AND WHY

Who we are:

Flame of Truth is a credited 501-C3, registered in the State of Texas since 1966. There are eighty churches founded under the ministry, and thirteen churches under our son Melvin Jr and his wife Rita's one-year mission work in Nicaragua, Central America.

Who we serve:

Flame of Truth Ministry was born to promote the gospel of Jesus Christ, reaching the lost at any cost. Assisting missionaries in other nations on and off the field. Providing opportunities for those desiring to experience short term mission work.

Why we serve:

To minister to the lost and hurting, to the sick and the poor. No one left behind.

Missionaries have told us that because of the assistance of Flame of Truth, they are still able to continue doing their missionary work. Their financial support had diminished, and it would have been impossible for them to continue without the support of Flame of Truth.

How we serve:

The Home Base is home of The Lighthouse Church where locals and visiting missionaries and mission groups can fellowship together.

We have a medical ministry in Mexico with Dr. Reyna meeting the needs of those families that cannot afford medical care.   Flame of Truth, with the help of the supporters, bought a property and built a medical clinic in Reynosa, Mexico and provided a Mobile Clinic that Dr Reyna can take on the road and assist the villages that do not have an office building to hold clinics in or setup after a disaster to care for the sick and injured.

There is an RV Park where missionaries can come out of Mexico to rest, relax, and fellowship with other missionaries. Stock up on needed supplies, get Visas renewed, etc. Many use the Home Base as their US mailing address. We supply them with Bibles, literature and tracks when available. We supply food, Video Schools in Spanish, and at times hold a Spanish course to help them learn or improve the language.

We provide a place where groups coming to work with the missionaries can stay. Even if a church group wanted to come to help on the mission field, but not sure what they wanted to do, we could always find something for them to do.   We could put them to work on the Home Base, maintaining the property and the facilities. We could take them to Mexico and arrange for churches where they could minister, with an interpreter provided, schedule a Bible School for the children, or they could build or do repair work on churches or a family home.

We have dormitories that can house up to eighteen men and eighteen women. There are six RV trailers available for families of two to five people. It includes a large Fellowship Hall with a kitchen for the groups to meet and feed their team. There is a laundromat on the property to take care of their dirty clothes, and shower rooms to clean up.

We offer office support for the missionaries, sending faxes, notarize papers, making copies, handling mail and banking, etc.

A food pantry that serves the missionaries and the needy in the local area. The food is purchased from donations from our ministry supporters.

Flame of Truth could not do all this without all the generous financial support from all our faithful supporters all these years. May God Bless you richly!!

References:

* Scripture references are all taken from the old King James Version (KJV)

* "Anabaptist Movement in 1525" can be found on the internet at:
Christianity Today – Christian History
https://www.christianitytoday.com/history/issues/issue-28/1525-anabaptist-movement-begins.html

* "Martyr's Mirror", book about the Holocaust. Book can be purchased online.

* Names used in this book, are by permission only.

Written by Melvin H. High, Sr
Edited by: Daughter, Sarah J. King
09-21-2018

For more copies of this book, contact us.

If the Lord lays it on your heart to support this Ministry, you can give a tax-deductible donation to Flame of Truth by mailing us at:

Flame of Truth
732 El Dora Rd,
Donna, TX 78537-5022

About the Author

Melvin H. High, Sr. born April 16, 1929
and married Sept. 25, 1948 to his wife Anna K Zook-High
They were called to the Mission Field in Mexico on January
7th of 1963 traveling 2000 miles with 9 little Missionaries, $6
in his pocket and a tank full of gas in a 1954 old rundown
Ford Station Wagon with all his family's belongings in tow
in a one- wheel trailer, and a faith that could move
mountains.

Melvin had an 8th grade education, customary in the
Mennonite/Amish faith, and went through
the school of hard knocks. He later went on to earn
his GED and three Doctorate Degrees.

April 16, 2019, he will be celebrating his ninetieth birthday.
Still going strong preaching the Gospel!

Made in the USA
Monee, IL
22 October 2021